YOUR GOD WON'T SAVE YOU

Pavan

ISBN-13: 9798674376415
ISBN-10: 1477123456

Cover design by: Art Painter
Library of Congress Control Number: 2018675309
Printed in the United States of America

*to Mother Nature and her
Magical Art of Evolution*

Going viral is not about reaching people's devices, it's about disturbing their perception on reality.

UNKNOWN

CONTENTS

On a rough sunny day, I read the following quote

"If you don't find a book that you want to read, you must be the one to write it"

That's it, the inspiration of this journey.

Your God Won't Save You

A BRIEF HISTORY OF MY CURSED LIFE

"The curse is a commodity for sale by theHuman tongue."

-by Ebola Virus

The first thing I did when I got liberated was to lose faith in Humanity, which you have already done. You, humans, are stupid, your world is Globalized and Modernized, right? It's just an arrogant belief, as my insight agitates to say that your world is Materialized. I find you so obstinate and obsessed that you are always on your way to prove your point over everything that appears in your sight. Your vision is demonized, and Renunciation turned out to be fiction after the parchment of paper notes. These printed notes have cajoled and influenced you to the extent that you have set foot to disrupt my Mother Nature. But my God just can't wait and watch this whole freaky show continue, and one day her abhorrence will rise up like a Phoenix and She'll lament on you in such a way that you'll never recover from the prolong pain, and your own Good God won't be there to save you. On the other hand, my liberation from the curse is just the beginning of the end.

I am Corona(by the way, we viruses don't have a name, and for your satisfaction, I am being called by the name you gave me) from the family of Viruses, and some of my brothers are Hanta, Ebola, Nipah, etc. I heard some so-called human professionals call me COVID-19, by which they mean to say is that I was first found in the year 2019. You imperfect human beings! I was there when the earth was devoid of animals, the time when Dinosaurs roamed like Kings and the time when Humans were still in the form of Naked Gorillas. I took birth around 1.5 billion years ago.

I witnessed Nature undergoing ablution to make this planet a better place to live and a favourable place, especially for you humans, who are the most sensitive animals of all animal kingdom. From the beginning of our life, we viruses were free from all constraints, we were a happy family with no perfect body but blessed with protein and genetic material. We were the most durable creatures that Mother Nature has ever procreated. Unlike other living beings we survived every possible threat from the beginning, we survived earthquakes, volcanoes, continental drifts, solar flares, magnetic storms, the magnetic reversal of the poles, thousands of years of bombardment by comets, meteors, and asteroids, worldwide floods, fires, erosion, cosmic rays, and recurring ice ages, etc. A virus's life is like a poison, it doesn't lose its property even if it expires. Our ability to survive and reproduce to any adhering environment was our strength, and this eventually turned out to be our weakness as Mother nature found that our presence in the free environment would make human life and its Evolution difficult. Her introspection made her believe in the procreation of Humans, whom she thought would take good care of her. This belief made her curse my family of deadly viruses and decided to lock us inside the body of some of her most trusted and adhering animals like bats, camels, dogs, etc. to whom we call our masters. I choose Bat....

She believed in you humans more than any animal she ever created, and made human Evolution in a perfect sense granting one of the powerful weapons called Brain and made it sophisticated enough to be self Conscious. You see through your eyes and your brain decides and interprets what you saw but what we microbes see will be in Singularity, we see the truth without any other versions of it, and the truth says that our Mother Nature regrets every bit of her decision made on the creation of your brain which was destined to be self-consciously turned out to be money conscious. Today you unworthy creatures who stand straight on your artificial clothes have put my mother in Jeopardy. You have turned this world into an artificial reality, the birds I used to see are now called as aeroplanes, the ants who swarmed the earth are replaced by smoke omitting cars and the towering trees with leaves now have windows and doors inhabited by you, squalor humans.

Two rocks produce spark and sound when they strike one another, but when the same rocks touches the water, it surrenders without any resistance,actually you are those rocks, and unfortunately, your spark instead of boiling the food turned out to be the forest fire. You will be thrown into the ocean one day, where you will lose all your ability and gradually you'll turn into the greasy soil of no use.

I once heard of your well-known scientist called Issac Newton and his law of action and reaction. It's so well written and universally accepted but just couldn't stop your cruel act of hunting and harming our Mother Nature and sometimes even in the name of your imaginative Good God, you commit unfathomable crimes. You, humans, are stern that you lack prudence in every aspect of your life. As a result of your ignorance, you have been facing threats every now, and then from floods, tsunamis, droughts, and even my brother Ebola came out of his curse, got liberated from his master gorilla, killing thousands of your kind in a landmass called Africa. I feel proud of him. It clearly shows you that the reaction to your horrendous crimes is always there, and I am part of this reaction being a pandemic with the help of your own connectivity between lands. Holes in the net cannot stop the wind coming inside, and you gotta remember that I am that fast blowing wind who will take off your neatly weaved net called community through connectivity.

The water in the ocean is squeezed into vapour when sunlight hits, but the same vapour turns back into rain one day and fulfils its life by supporting plants on the land. Nobody's held back and tied under the rule of Nature, everyone gets their chance, and everything happens for a reason, there are no accidents, and I am here to quote my reasons, I am here, to tell the truth, the truth that you knew but never took time to reflect. The truth about your corrupt actions over Nature, from your false beliefs to pure Stupidity.

Its time for you to take a tour of reality through the perspective of a virus. You know what? Truth can be clearly seen when seen through 5 different perspectives; and I eagerly want you to listen to my viewpoint, which can carry a more significant mass on things as they lie around. My journey around your household will give you a much more unobstructed view about your unknown Stupidity in a way that you have never imagined it to be. I have thought of meeting all those microbes living around you, which includes my friend bacteria and my virus family. Let's start the journey about analyzing and accepting truth through the perspective of a Deadly Virus.

Before getting started, if you are dumb enough to have believed that the Chocolate milk comes from a brown cow, don't go further...

THE SOCIAL EXPERIMENT.

"God is just an idea that unites and divides people"

-- Spanish flu

The Social Experiment

Y ou, Humans, are very interesting, Nature assigned you the same red blood but your innate fiendish efficacy which is to be superior over every other being led you to differentiate yourselves under the name of sex, color, religion, and social status.

When you throw a stone to a dog and a lion, a lion always reattacks, but a dog just barks and runs away. Just like that, Lion, you are when the science people like Darwin deny the existence of your God. Eventually, you'll turn out to be a dog when someone speaks of the Integrity of Humans across the globe. Ignoring the true God as Nature, you believe in your imaginative God living in the clouds by expecting the miracle to happen anytime. On the darker side, you guys lock your over-imaginative fellow beings inside the prison, tagging them as psychopaths. If I was allowed to claim the powers which could control and punish you humans, I would have sternly taken out an organ from your body every time you people bowed your heads looking at your feet in front of your supernatural God believing that it would solve your problem out of nowhere all the while ignoring and exploiting the true God Nature. This behavior forces me to conclude that you humans, the so-called intelligent species are just literate enough to read and write scriptures but not Educated in any way to understand the sole truth. Pigs would sound better if they spell ABCD.

Science is the only thing on earth that deserves the respect of my virus family and all of the animal kingdom as it accepts and preaches the Evolution, the magic created by Nature, the only true God on earth.
You got to pray what's true, not what you believe to be true.

The rock stays like a rock until the water and weather hit it so hard and so often that it will one day turn itself into a beautiful shape or become soil that starts to support plants. Just like the rock, I think you humans need the hit from the Evolution many times and to the right part(brain) until you unlearn everything about your God and start believing in yourselves. I am not roasting you because of your belief in your God, sometimes some of you do good deeds by fearing God, but at the same time, you would end up denying the sole truth of your existence claiming that your God to be the only answer.

The religion on which you have the conceit of has no base, it has aggravated your thinking system enclosed inside your skull, if you go on claiming that GOD is the only reason for all creation on earth, you are already out of the way to understand science and Evolution.

It's not possible that there's no beautiful lotus in between a dirty pond. One among you who called himself as Geroge Carlin impressed me by stating boldly that "Religion has actually convinced people that there's an invisible man living in the sky who watches everything you do, every minute of every day. And the invisible man has a special list of ten things he does not want you to do. And if you do any of these ten things, he has a special place, full of fire and smoke and burning and torture and anguish, where he will send you to live and suffer and burn and choke and scream and cry forever and ever

'til the end of time! But He loves you. He loves you, and He needs money! He always needs money! He's all-powerful, all-perfect, all-knowing, and all-wise, somehow just can't handle money! ".
 Mother Nature is proud of him. This man is so wise to be called Educated, as I was lucky to hear this speech when I was still a prisoner inside my master Bat, who accidentally went flying inside an auditorium where you humans were ironically laughing with your full breadth belching continuously to actual facts.' One can witness the beautiful rainbow only when the sun stands against rainfall. This man was the bright sun born in between the empty heads of darkness'.

On my way on earth, I met a bacteria, who is my all-time family friend and the one who domiciles beside you, from your toothbrush to your coffin. He knew more about you humans than any other organism on earth. He was none other than Salmonella, who had expertise in making you sick by entering your body through your long-kept food. We greeted each other, and the moment I asked about you humans, he was turned up and became enthusiastic about you and said,
"what can I say because I can't just sacrifice my whole life explaining these creatures. But, I can say this for sure. Human mind and mood takes more

number of shape than my family members do" we both laughed down and as we were standing on your food and we were about to enter inside your stinking stomach, so I decided to move to some other place and take a tour around your homes to which Salmonella gladly agreed.

The only thing that had spread between humans more than bacteria and viruses combined was ignorance. If I were to believe in human God, I would spend the next few centuries in choosing the God who matches my lifestyle, principles, and purposes. Wait! Is there a God for viruses too? What do you call him/her? Virus BABA?

We roamed around your neighborhood, your parks, public toilets, parking lots, etc., we were tired after this brief checkout and decided to rest, and we both sat on an ant expecting that it would take us to it's mud home where we could have a chance to meet Staphylococcus who was our long lost cousin germ. Being interrupted by a human who was walking by, the ant unknowing carried us on his leg which was covered with some hard, shiny cloth on it to which you called as a shoe. We had no other option but to hold on, and this human entered into a very strange place where you people were true to yourselves and helped each other get up in their life. Unfortunately, it was not a temple, mosque, or a church. I was confused at first sight and as I took my sight towards Salmonella for an explanation he turning towards me said "its a bar, the place where human goes out of control,"

"how do you know exactly?"

"I have been inside that bottle many times."

"what's in that bottle ?"

"its liquor, the liquid that humans created for their entertainment, They say that its harmful and this is the same drink which is saving a human government to function properly with their paper money. "

I took a look around again looking all those sober faces with spilled liquor on their shirts and pants and then I got to know why it was harmful, it's harmful because, it makes you speak the truth and you humans never like the truth, as truth carries the power of reality it can turn you down in front of one another. You humans seek pleasure at both from the drink as well as from lies.
As we were still on the leg, a drop of beer fell on us when the human who was carrying us bumped another accidentally, the splash hit us so hard that I fell unconscious and when I woke up I was inside a big box(dustbin), and I found myself scrapped inside a white paper(tissue paper) and when I searched for Salmonella, he was not there, I was tensed and worried, I needed him to assure my way out of there. I was left without hope inside a big litter box. When I was high on tension, then I saw

some Salmonella's enemy lysozymes, they were busy killing bacterias they saw on sight, even they entered that litter box through tissue paper as they actually resided in your saliva all the time. Finally, I saw a cockroach approaching towards me, and there he was, Salmonella riding on its back.

"come on my friend, let's go for a ride out," he said

I was happy to find him, and we both ran out on a cockroach's back, cheering our goodbye to one of the honest places on earth. THE BAR.
I took Salmonella and his network around your household for granted and sought out to find the reason behind your faith and devotion to your God. This game of exploration was about to give us a too great experience, and both of us decided to begin this crazy expedition from your Bandage center (Hospital). When we moved in the scenes there were very heartbreaking, I never thought I would feel empathy, but there I felt after looking at those patients who lost their legs, hands, and sometimes heads too.
It's straightforward to convince someone who has negligible knowledge of the world around, and everyone of you were there in that Bandage center during your birth, the one who got convinced without any prior knowledge of the surrounding.

Just 5 minutes after your birth, your parents decide your name, nationality, religion, and sect, and you being the victims spends the rest of your life, defending something that you never choose. It's like feeding the newborn baby with all the toxic food, thinking that one day the baby will grow up to take care of the guardian. Heartfelt thanks to Salmonella, who told me that there are about 1400 religions on earth with their own rules, rituals, and Gods. These 1400 religions add up to 1400 gods, only if I consider one God from each religion.

If you believe in one among them, Why aren't these gods protecting you from me? If he can do miracles in the holy books, why isn't he taking action against me? Is he afraid of me, or is he busy doing chemistry with the chemicals he claimed to have created to invent a vaccine against me? When it's prepared has he thought of throwing the vaccine as holy water from the year-old saucers used by his earthly contractors?. The God that you claim to be present is just an idea like a movie character saving the innocent and kicking the ass of villains. Your God just unites familiar minded people just like the presence of RNA and DNA unites us as viruses. Nature is the only true God, it gives you air to breathe, water to drink and cleanse, food to eat, fire to cook, and shelter to live safely. The only purpose of God is to show kindness, which is all the while done by Nature itself from the birth of Humanity.

Until Nature arrives to render help, the only ones who can help and save your ignorant literate humans from me are the Scientists and Doctors. The ones who teach Evolution as the grand concept behind the creation of living beings. Let's consider my pandemic as a social experiment. An experiment to arbitrate if you humans are still dumb enough to rely on your religion and God instead of actual warriors who believe in Science to find a cure. How did you humans even think that there is an omnipotent being living in the sky procreated a dog saying "you will be man's best friend, you will bark, you will live up to 13 years, you will go on mating other breeds of your kind and one day end up lying in a human's home not doing anything but to piss on the same rock every day".

Let us assume that your God (if exists) accidentally lands on earth on his way to some distant galaxy to light the supernova. If he meets any of you humans on the road, the only one thing that both of you would say to each other is, "I created you". Even before you get into this conversation, there's no doubt that you would make an attempt to ask Identification of his religion, caste, and demographics.

Goddess Nature never felt the need to understand the word Prejudice, so does the people with a microscope in their hand and science in their mind, who work for the betterment of Humanity. Of course, they fight against me, and sometimes they don't believe in Nature as a true God too, but at least they believe in the creation of Nature and use their brain on some divine purpose instead of going underground claiming that there's a God to take care of.

Never have I thought that I would be procreating myself inside the bodies of yours and then moving to one another.

In the process of my infection, one fine day I accidentally fell on a luminous screen with colorful blocks moving with the swipes of your fingers, they called that animal as SmartPhone(by the way it was not an animal if it were, no doubt it would have taken over Humanity by now), I was shocked in the beginning to think that Nature never created any rectangular animal with more intelligence than humans, but after observing the actions performed over it I realized how lazy and hopeless you humans are, to create something that would avowedly do your work without excuses. You humans, have turned out to be parasites, but this time it's you who are inured on this rectangular luminous being. I was lying on this Smartphone for a week, and the one who was using it was most of the time entering into the world of a bluebird with Twitter written below it, one day I noticed something inside it that went like #stayhomestaysafe and wondered that it was actually an order for everyone to follow, but that man was hanging out of his home pressing the heart icon and typing some comments on the same topic. Not just the bluebird, he did the same on some other virtual worlds called by the name Instagram, Facebook, and Reddit. He never took the signs of warning seriously; the only sign he took seriously was the sign which popped out of nowhere, saying "WARNING! BATTERY LOW".

I feel loathed every time I remember the frittenful act on the device. It is a technology built by you which instead of being invented is getting adopted. I sometimes hear that your great God is both omnipotent and omniscient, and I am very happy for you to announce that your God always resides in your own hand. Yes! That rectangular luminous screen is omniscient, which can answer all your queries, be it an emotional problem or a normal one, and the day is fast appraching that it would be omnipotent with your won help. But at that time, it won't just answer and help you, but control you with all your algorithms and technological power.

The waterfalls always entertain the viewers, but in the end, the water always flows down to towards the earth; never does it follies to be at the top of the land. But you humans are entertainment seekers, never giving up your self esteem to something that can bring you down, you are so light-minded and are consequently exposed to the fictional comics and the characters in it, thinking that there will be someone in the form of Superman or Captain America, would someday arrive for help. But you ignorant beings never make an attempt to be a superhero. The truth is that your rectangular screens have actually exulted the freedom as a human being, especially the freedom of expression, which is provided by your constitution. Just like your constitution and with laws, there are rules of nature that each and every animal lives every second following them and its time to remind you of the rules that you have no idea of, here are they

1.Freedom of habitat
2.Freedom to hibernate.
3.No overconsumption of food
4.Freedom over water bodies
5.Exclusive territories for all animals
6.Trust in mutual existence
7.Everybody after death must degrade and give rise to a new plant.

That's not it, there is a punishment for those who violate these rules, and it would be better if I introduce you to the animals who met the penalty instead of the punishment they faced. THE DINOSAURS FAMILY. And I am Goddamn sure that you are the next in that list with the red underline.

A monkey always resides in a tree, that doesn't mean that it won't like to sleep inside a Lion's den, it means it knows its limits and respects other animals territory. But you are those developed monkeys who are going to get eaten by the hungry lion for taking a chance to fulfill your stupid pleasure of sleeping in its den.

If I get any chance to meet Nature one day, I will recommend it to add one more rule stating

"NO FRIENDSHIP WITH HUMANS and DON'T BELIEVE IN HUMAN GOD"

Affection shows your mentality, but only the situation reveals reality. From the time I was liberated, even my thinking was human-like filled with selfishness and obstinate not to give up on my family, but unlike humans, I was right about my self and my thoughts all the time, and I am right.

Of course, I have no affection, but the situation is different, for you are the one to be blamed for my behavior, and your mentality is the sole reason for my outbreak. There's a saying that one of you had quoted which goes by "life has no limitation except the one you make". why don't you humans just understand this and stay in your limits, here I am being your limit on your own world, killing your own beings without mercy. I won't end my story until I make you understand what made me do things that I do.

You are a human, and you live with your beings, but

the truth is you don't, you are absolutely unaware of yourselves. As a result, most of your beliefs about your behavior are always wrong. One thing that I love about you humans is your ability to create art, especially poetry. My messiah William Wordsworth stands as a pillar behind my education, he was the first among you to come up with a religion praying our Nature as a true god. Now that me being his follower, I believe that it's my duty to write a poem and give him a tribute.

◆ ◆ ◆

Thou shall live, and thou shall not believe,
In someone who gazes from the sky.
You're worried about pandemic ignoring
the Pandemonium,
Of who the hell built that ladder so high.

If the hell is burning down,
And heaven is floating above.
What's the difference human?
While you're the only Psychopaths around.

What a world this is,
Where prayers are fiendish than friendly,
If someone did hear them,
He would have stripped his ears,
leaving prayers to go gypsy.

I am not the only skeptic here,
For you can join my team.
don't be weak, just stay scrupulous
For morose voices soon be seen.

THE PROTEIN FACTOR

"The food is always free by the Nature, but the only ones who pay for it are called as Human Beings"

-- Small Pox

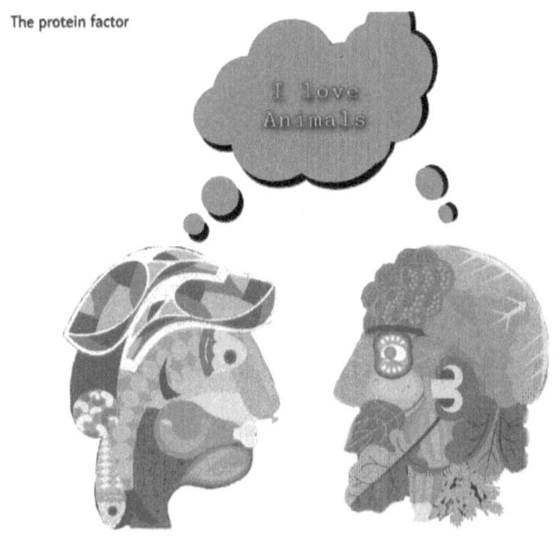

Human nature is humorous, the word HUMAN what Nature meant while procreating you is Highly Understandable Mankind According to Nature, but when I think about it, it totally falls under contradiction, you Humans are Highly Unconditional Mentals with Abusive Nature. The facts are actually funnier than jokes on you people.

One of these facts is that if the Animals around you fight for food, you dire Humans fight with food. Food is equally distributed, but it depends on the thought of those who consume it. When Mother Nature was still planning on the creation of human evolution, her prudence about your palate made her grant a more considerable reproductive power to all the possible consumable animals. It was her kindness towards you not scorching abhorrence towards other animals.

A bird will throw its babies out of the nest as soon as it discovers its wings. But Nature made you stay safe considering you as delicate beings, providing you the perfect condition for evolution. But all the while, you were hungry vultures. It's tough to believe that you humans find greater happiness and joke witnessing not just a dead animal, even the death of your own beings brings great interest to you. You think of killing as if you were made for it, beginning from video games you run to the extent of war between land masses with a flag of your own.

I believe that if slaughterhouses had glass walls, then everyone would have given up eating animals. You are the bloody murderers. How would you feel if the Rhino chip out your nose? Imagine an elephant sawing out your teeth. Would you bear the pain if a tiger scrapes out your skin? How can you behave very easily while you cut the body of a calf in front of its own tear shedding mother?

I was there when the former happened inside the rumen of the cow, which was standing on the ocean of its own tears. I was there with 100billion bacteria, 10million protozoa, and 10 thousand fungi sharing the worst time with me.

"every time they say something they mean the opposite," said the bacteria weeping with its breadth out "we worked hard to produce the purest of milk for its baby. I can't stand here watching this happen anymore, I am going to complain to our Judge Pigeon?"

"We took great care of the calf just like its own mother while it saw still inside the stomach, we fed it with all the nutrients we obtained from the cud, but now all our love is being cut down into pieces," said the protozoa sharing its unfathomable pain with bacteria.

It was fungi who didn't cry; it came facing directly towards me looking into my eyes, he said, putting all his pain out.

"I know you have your own limits, but don't let it

give time for these humans to find a vaccine against you. I want you to kill all of these haughty humans one by one. Kill a kid in front of its own parent so that they'll get to know what every cow goes through "

I was speechless as I was still in pain, and I could clearly witness the neurotransmitters inducing depression, grief and anxiety were busy flooding the whole body of the cow. It was having the worst time suffering for something that it never had control of.

If this is the story of a single cow, what would be the fate of the whole Cow family on earth?

When you construct a new home, you'll allow a cow to enter first so that it would bring you good luck, but you'll end up eating its own meat at the same home. You pray cow and consider it as the holy animal where your God lives, but you'll end up drinking its milk meant for its calf. Unfortunately, this harassment on these speechless animals is taken as the act of superiority. A fish always stays inside the water; neither does it drink water nor leave the water because it believes in its belonging there. But you have both exploited nature and left it damaged like it never belonged to you. Your muscles grow when you consume the flesh, when will you build your brain and try to absorb and understand the pain by these voiceless animals who are serving you without anything in return?

You humans turn out to be emotional while speaking of death, especially when a baby dies in front of a parent. If so, how can you let an egg be consumed every day as a breakfast which contains a precious life?

If your government punishes you for killing a deer, why don't it punish you for eating a chicken, sheep, or a cow? All I can say about your government is that it lacks common sense and it is tied up with an infinite thread called stupidity; according to your stupid government with its biased laws, a chicken's life is less important to be consumed than the life of deer. How dare it is to make laws that encourage to cut off the head of animals with life inside. If animals could talk, the only universal thing that your ears could grasp is criticism and hatred. I know you are so smart to criticize my own words stating the behavior of wild animals eating each other? Remember, wild animals hunt other animals just to ease their sensation of hunger, and it would never ever think about storing meat or taming it for future consumption. If a tiger hunts a deer, it will never carry the leftover beef to its cave, it would leave the place, and a hyena or some small carnivores will consume it. But you are so obsessed with your idiotic stupidity that you ended up doing business out of it. Everything has a limit; unfortunately, you people are awarded to think out of the box and to store food inside your cooling machines, ignoring a beggar and a street dog in front of your home who have eaten nothing for days.

There are some of you whom I almost forgot to mention, the vegans. When I first heard about these people, I thought that they invented their own food from non-living things like mud, air, and water, but they actually consumed green leaves again, taking away life. If non-vegetarians kills cow by consuming its meat, vegans kill a cow by consuming its grass on the land. You, Humans, are all the same, and only one thing that separates within yourself is the excess of stupidity. All humans are stupid, those with less stupidity cause 0.0000000001% less harm to Mother Nature than those who live a completely stupid lives.

The lessons to this stupidity begin at your schools, where you learn from books that are made up to reduce your critical thinking ability than the books that broaden your mind towards Nature. Its the same school where they will teach you to be non-violent and maintain peace and harmony with Nature. But you have almost forgotten that the school you study in is built burying thousands of trees for land and for your paper damaging crores of habitat. If this is the irony of your school, how can I accept you as an enlightened being? As I said earlier, you are literate, not educated. A pig would sound better if it spelled ABCD.

As animals' consumption went on high, the threat was seen to be slightly diluted when Nature filled the gap by filling the idea of farming into your brains by giving some positive signs of seeds and fertile land.

Agriculture is the wisest pursuit, as it leads to the real wealth that is morality and happiness within you. A night star brings a smile to the viewers with its blinking traits, but these stars disappear with the smile when the sun hits the sky. Just like that, gradually, when paper money stood on pulpit, these happy humans don't turn out to be farmers, but the businessmen selling their products. Farmers are the only trustworthy humans who are in harmony with nature, they are one of the purest souls whose friendship extend out of humanity, bees help them in pollination, bulls help them in plowing and harvesting, earthworms help them in fertilizing, and Goddess Nature blesses them with regular rainfall and sunlight. When I roamed around your highly sophisticated marketplace with Salmonella earlier, farmer's true worth was disguised, all the products of Nature were found with the money tag below them. Freshwater freely available in the rivers, ponds, and lakes are now sold in packed plastic bottles, the healthy fruits which blither on trees are now made as sugar water and named under some corporation with no credits to the cabal of Mother Nature.

Most importantly, the animals that are meant to be living with their families in some forest and neighborhood are now sold under KFC's, Mcdonalds, and Burger King. Nature is for sale, and the secret of selling is 'sincerity,' and once they fake that, they are made up for the job. They tell the truth, always the truth but not the whole truth, and the entire truth found me when I watched a tiny man speaking through that rectangular screen who came out through a red rectangular block with a white triangle inscribed in the middle of it called Youtube.

He said that my brothers and I are causing the disease called Zonotonic diseases, which means we are the fugitives of the animals living around and out of human habitat. He gave a interesting number, that 60% of infectious diseases are Zonotonic. I was worried that the man explaining all these things would conclude by blaming the animals as haughty and morose, but he was the man of science and evolution, and he proudly took our side, happiness inside me was at its best. He intensified my mind and cleared all of my doubts by stating the reason behind my family's liberation. The reason was you, Humans, all the time, your disruption and connections, that revile road leading you to the modern world created this havoc of my liberation from my master Bat.

As I continued watching over youtube, the man who was watching the videos turned out to be a man of infinite stupidity. The following videos really blew my mind away. Here's the list of them

How to kill yourselves without bleeding by beating your shadow with a stick

How to read a book without opening it

How to speak to a dog using a cat

How to invent the time machine and surprise your parents in their marriage.

How to get inside a snails shell and have a coffee break.

If this was the case of the man watching it, what about those who made these

Mother nature equally distributed each and every component that supports the lifelike carbohydrates, protein, vitamin, fats, etc. You are so obstinate that you always need more, as the highest fatality in human nature is greed and selfishness, as a result, in search of protein, fats and, vitamins found in other animals flesh, it is influencing your quackery behavior to hunt and kill those animals totally unaware of my families existence inside their body. I always feel lucky about my family and me for being microscopic with a protein-rich body. If we were of Frog's size, our flesh would have been bathing in your stomach's acid and meeting bacteria inside the human intestine following the road towards your toilet room. I am here not because of my vengeance, but because of your ignorance.

I am here to restore the animal kingdom's protein level by giving a small amount of lament to you, but the whole story opens up when Goddess nature opens up her abhorrence.

Animals and forests can survive without you, but you can never breathe a bit without forests. Every forest has been injected with roads and your machines with no life while drinking that dirty oil are killing animal lives which were meant to balance the ecosystem, if there was even a bit of conscious in these vehicles without a doubt they would have loathed on your actions. Your brain is developed, you can think twice, you can analyze the situation. If you can get afraid of sudden fire, flood, and earthquake, just think about the animals whose only source of thoughts that are visceral (to fight or to flee), how much fear they might go through when they see a rough jeep fast approaching towards them.

It is just 2%, the difference between you and a chimpanzee. It may appear as a small number, but the difference it made is so vast that it began with a wheel built with the rock to the space station that will never crack. You, humans, are all different; your cultures are different, and so is your lifestyle. If a tiger walks naked, your lifestyle demands its skin to cover your body. If a fish is a free underwater, your culture forces you to fry it to be free from hunger. Your trust with nature is demolished; no animals trust you. By the way, how can you expect an animal to trust you when you won't believe in your own beings. You, humans, are so out of your mind that you get separated with your opposite sex just because of snoring while sleeping, you are thrown out of your work, just because of one's long nose. Your fundamental nature sucks, but you are all ready to talk about globalization. You can't even repair your faults, some of your beings at the age of 6 are laborers, are getting married at that early age, and your female beings are abused and harassed without mercy. Nature never created you for these stupid acts. Grow Up.

Sometimes I feel disgusted witnessing some of you with boards and signs written with "Save forests" and "Save Air," claiming to be environmentalists and animal saviors. I was happy to know about these groups, but I was struck dumb when I saw the board was written with" "save the earth." How stupid ! you are always foolish and will be silly till the end of time, you don't know how to take care of oneself and care for one another, but here you are standing on a small street of beside stinky sewage, ready to save the whole big planet which is more than a billion trillion times bigger than you?. These kinds of people are actually of very little importance with little impact on animal life. They are just attention seekers who protest for some time as a timepass on a dreary day. I think you humans must spend more time buying a bed and thinking if your bedroom has become small or big instead of destroying nature with your over-imaginative thoughts.

Books are said to be your greatest invention, as noted by Salmonella and most of my family members. I always wanted to explore books as I heard my brothers and especially my grandfather Spanish flu was recorded inside them, It was a great day as I ended up landing inside your public library through the cockroach and was admirably lucky not to get eaten by a rat as I got stuck to a unique book while the rat chased down the cockroach. The book's front cover was a pig wearing a soldier uniform. Pigs are considered as one of the smartest species as blessed by Mother Nature with their cute snort. I couldn't wait but to read the book "Animal Farm by George Orwell."

Tears rolled down as I read word by word when the farm was captured by animals lead by Pig. Unfortunately, it ended up bad for animals, but as I reminiscence that it was written by a human, I was relieved. It was Ok, A human would always write in favor of humans. I always pray to Mother Nature for the story to come true with humans replacing Animals in the farm and name it as

"Human Farm by Gorgeously Natural "

There are some of you who are ready to hurt an animal, throw stones at dogs, kill rats with poison, and kill snakes even if it's just moving away seeking its eggs laid somewhere around. The following story said by Rabies virus is an excellent example that animals are much mature when it comes to emotions.

I met rabies inside the saliva of a dog, which was spitted on the street when I came out of the library through the lizard, which was lazily lying on the wall, unable to read those books.

Rabies began.

The dog where I was present was pregnant and had a severely wounded leg and was lying on the roadside. One day some old lady took it home and fed it with proper food and gave some medication. The dog was doing great until that old lady's son arrived, he was a human doctor, he saw the pregnant dog as a threat to their health and hygiene and decided to leave the dog somewhere else, confronted by his mother, he stood back. When the dog delivered 5 babies, one of them died soon after entering the world, and among these four, both the doctor and his mother decided to care for only one baby, and I was lucky to be inside the baby they took care of. What happened to other babies was unknown to the dog where I was present. I have once heard the doctor saying his mother about leaving the other dogs near the sewage dump. The dog staying in the house was disappointed in the doctor, and it took no interest in him, but it loved his mother, who took care of it like her own child. Everything went on sound for the dog, but one day, the doctor came with a lady claiming her to be his wife, his mother was both shocked, and happy.she welcomed her wholeheartedly. After some days, we heard some quarreling sound coming from the house, which indicated the fight between the doctor's wife and his mother. It was a terrible day when the doctor took his mother to someplace where old people live. The dog was unfortunate, and after some days the dog escaped the home and went towards that old lady, on that way I fell on this street here. You know whats an exciting part of the story. look at that tree over there, and the paper nailed to it, it has the dogs picture, and there's something written below it

"Lost DOG! The reward of 25000 will be given to the informant."

With all his heart, he pointed his
clasped palms towards the sky.

Farmer's lustrous eyes bestow gratitude
for all the shower of love on the dry.

Wheatfields shine and reflect the
golden glow of the dawn,

Wealth gets bungled once put into the
hands of a wolfish businessman.

Maligned into a hamburger packed
for an obese's happy burp,

May he starve, but nutrition? Nope..!!

*The calf gets its first leisurely stroll
and a happy green farm browse,*

*Little does it know it's its way to
the slaughterhouse.*

Domesticated, Fed and fattened for a juicy steak,

*Hardly any happier life than the black
rhino in extinction's peak*

Dear man, Karma ought to return all your favors,

*Now morphed as me who feeds on
your life in all flavors.*

◆ ◆ ◆

THE PLASTIC PURPOSE

"The only everlasting thing that humans created is plastic"

-- SARS

Plastic Purpose

Y ou, humans, are insolent, the more you think you people are developed, the more the fire burns behind your back, you have almost forgotten that peace is the only greatest weapon for development that any animal can achieve. Your arrogance and the ability to speak made you believe that you are the genius, you should know that the only difference between genius and stupidity is that a genius always has its limits. When it comes to you, forget limits, you can't even figure out what differentiates between an optimist and a pessimist. I always feel pity about that unsolved half filled or half empty cup problem. The answer to your age-old half empty or full glass problem is that it always depended on your last action with it. If you drank from it, its half-empty but if you filled it, it's half full. Now, this is what I call a genius answer. A genius always thinks laterally, but your thinking does end up with collateral damage either to your own mind or your surrounding. You're stupid enough to believe that the Sea water is salty because of fish's tears. You know what? You are turning it as a reality with your plastic.

A good day for my virus family is the day when we reduce the mass of ego off this planet by infecting and killing organisms that inhale air and exhale blame. It was a great day for me as I made my way infecting through thousands of you which initiated tiredness and made me sleepy in between the way of millions. When I woke up I was lying there inside your body, the second most stinky part, the large intestine (the first place is already secured and won by your Brain). Inside the large intestine, the habitation of lactobacillus bacteria, one of my closest friends was about to be reunited. Happiness and bacteria have one thing in common, they multiply by dividing.

Lactobacillus came running towards me, waving his hand with some stinky fluid stuck over it. I wondered and appreciated its unique capacity to live in such a harsh and stinky place ever found on earth, if any of you stayed in such kind of place even for a minute, you would be going for a strike against your government with a board saying, "we need clean water to drink not shit to eat". It was a bad place to have a conversation with someone whom you meet after thousands of centuries. I thought of taking him to the stomach, but he declined warning me seriously about the presence of acid in your stomach, which would have killed both of us in an instant flush. There was no other way but to greet him at that very place, but there was something very unusual with him that day. He showed something and asked me about it, as he amusingly said that he had never witnessed anything like that appear in the large intestine ever before. After cleaning it with some unknown fluid, I concluded that the material he was unaware of was actually Plastic. Yes! The same plastic that you need for holding a bottle of rum to the night condoms.

"It's plastic, my friend," I said

"Is it the same plastic that our Goddess nature wanted for ages?"

"I'm sorry what? Did you say mother nature wanted it?" I asked as my receptors got lightened up at that very instant while the whole stinky surrounding switched as a void space, leaving space only for his words to be heard. Washing his hand he replied with the whole new story of plastic that I had never heard before, it sounded so idiotic and funny, while on the other hand it ironically answered one of the greatest philosophical questions that intelligent you ask yourselves on the sleepless midnight "why are we here?".

The story began when the world began when mother nature procreated earth with its vast diversity in landmass, forest area and water resources she even brought life into it starting from single-celled organisms which evolved into multicellulars and even gave differentiating characters to each of the evolved species so that the world will be a beautiful place to have a tour of. Goddess nature loved all her children, but the problem came during crises like earthquakes, floods, tsunamis which partnered with meteor attacks. All these beautiful creatures perished which left Goddess Nature to stay in solitude until a worthy being shows of itself being survived from the destruction. We microbes were there all this time, but Nature ignored us considering our size which made her think of Plastic, the thing that would stay forever with nature, the thing that would convert the earth into a new paradigm called Eartholastic, the combination of Earth and Plastic. By the way, it was the evil Volcano's curse on our Nature, when Nature denied its existence. Volcano brainwashed Nature to think that plastic-type substance which erupted from it will one day grow up to save the earth from all the bad animals stating that all the bad animals would die immediately after eating plastic. She never had any idea of its creation, which made her create a brain to deal with it and made humans who could fit themselves inside the brain. Today the one and only purpose of humans is to produce plastic.

"Finally, I found it, my friend, a human purpose is fulfilled," said Lacto excitedly.

"If their purpose is met, why are they still living? Do you know what happened to our grandfather Spanish flu? He finished his job and got extinct" I said.

"I thought that's the reason you are killing these humans, it can't be true that you are liberated accidentally without any purpose, your purpose is to kill those whose purpose is fulfilled," Lacto said. I evacuated the intestine without continuing the conversation as it was too awful to portray myself as a messiah and mainly to have a talk at that kind of place with a bacteria who went on bowing in front of me without a pause.

I came out of there, and for once I thought about the way you people divide yourselves under many names, let me tell you something when I was in your body, I found only two types of humans, the ones with the extended part between thighs and ones who lacked. Is that what you call gender? Let me remind you of something very important. Gender shouldn't be considered as a social construct, just look at all those animals around you, after running through your markets I found that gender is actually a scam made up by the bathroom companies to sell more bathrooms. Do you see any other animals in the whole earth which differentiates itself under the name of gender, or does any animal claim a separate place to expel the filtered component out of its body?

I was stuck with the idea of plastic and the story of Lacto, and for a compliment on these thoughts, there I saw plastic on streets, lakes, homes, trees, soil, oceans and interestingly I even found plastic inscribed inside human skin, which was used to mould their skin to look extraordinary. How immature!

There are 4 fastest networks in your world.
1.Telecom
2.Television
3.Tell a woman(said by rabies virus, blame him)
4.Thrash production

You are aware that the plastic you toss away enters the ocean, and then into the fish and ends up on your own plate, but still, you do it. If Nature had really wanted plastic, it was a bad decision to create you for it, even apes could have done it. The whole system looks like a waste animal producing tons of waste and pouring that waste into the ocean killing its inhabitants and in the first place plastic is also a combination of unused waste chemical just like your brain. The plastic in the ocean is creating great trouble with increasing mass, but here you are busy and lost in the world of music with less treble and more bass to a song called "Don't blame me!". The people who are selling you these plastics are the ones who are legally taking away the good future of the earth.

If it continues at this rate, it's no surprise that one day you'll be picked up as a thrash to the environment by Goddess Nature. And if the Goddess Nature gave speaking power to Plastic, it would have responded you in your own words saying "roses are red, violets are blue, if I had five fingers the middle one's for you". Even the plastic would go against you unable to stand the rate of its consumption and getting ended up in an ocean.

 I say that you gotta avoid plastic because its the only planet in this universe with less of my family members. How would you feel if a portion of food gets stuck in your throat for a minute, you'll visit the gate of death at that very moment in time. Imagine animals getting their whole body stuck inside and out with plastic hopping their precious lives between life and death until the end of time, unable to swallow and spit out. You have your doctors to operate, just think about those animals out there. First of all, do you even know what happens to the plastic after you kick throw it inside the dustbin, how would you know? When you lack the simple difference between recycling and reusing.

You can't expect a tree to stop growing just by cutting its branches and removing all its leaves, you gotta reach its roots, likewise your reduced use and ban on plastic is just like removing the dried up leaves from a big-year-old mature tree with deep roots attached to money, you have to take out its roots or else the whole universe remembers you as the species who killed their own beings not by their hand but by some shitty non-degradable thing called plastic. A matchstick is enough to burn the paper containing the artwork created with extreme passionate efforts for many years, just like that matchstick, your plastic is destroying the magical art of evolution by killing millions of species on the ocean which were meant to balance the ecosystem. A spoonful of ocean water contains, thousands of my family members and friends, now your 1rupee plastic is injecting with toxic chemicals so sternly that it perishes out all those microbes who were supporting the lives of marine animals.

Earth has been here from around 4.5 billion years and you humans are here for just around 2.5 million years, and you have been into these heavy industries for only around 250 to 300 years, and these 250 years have made earth such a devastating place that these 4.5 billion years have never witnessed, there's plastic everywhere, and there is pollution everywhere. The clean air is polluted, the water is contaminated, and the land has been spoiled just because of your greed, if dinosaur lived, there would be very less mess except their shit lying around. Then comes the deforestation which reduces the purest part of nature called a forest, which ultimately forces the animals to enter the violent human zone and get themselves killed without mercy. How ironic it is to cut trees for papers and writing over them to stop cutting trees. It really is a freaky show that is going on with your lives. It has no signs of an end. Before the Goddess Nature arise to kill humans, I will do my best to reduce her burden. You turned your whole godamn life into a game of committing sin and judging sinners who sinned differently. As soon as your road to commit sin comes to an end you are all wise to take up the different route of abusing the weaker section of your own kind, just like charging a man with no arms in the name of stabbing his son.

You, humans, are filling the space every second on this earth, if you are allowed to continue to rule the world at this pace, genetic engineering, permutation and combination of the count on superior genius genes mismatches and the passage of time will be your community alone called "Superhumans", who probably will be able to prolong life indefinitely producing more plastic and pollution, you'll combat my family and one day can even conquer incurable diseases.

A butterfly seeks and sucks nectar from every flower it encounters, but it never forgets to return its favour by completing pollination promoting its growth over different places. Here you are taking away everything you can from Nature without returning your favour, Nature never wanted you to give up your worldly things instead to plant some saplings, just once in your lifetime. If I get any chance to meet my family members residing inside the butterfly, I would suggest them to redirect the whole butterfly community to start flapping its wings initiating tornado at every corner of the world.

There has never been a day in my life watching a bacteria cry. It was Ideonella Sakaiensis for whom we called as Saken with respect. Saken and his family are the micro warriors of Nature, they are famous for their ability to break down some of your dirty plastic. Every microbe on this planet had great respect for them. I was glad to meet such honourable bacteria, and I took great pride in me to have a conversation with him.

"How are you, my friend, it's my honour to meet you," I said excitedly.

"my pleasure, corona," he said with disguised pain in his voice.

Me: "what happened, my friend, everything all right?"

Saken: "How can I tell you this? ...it's been months since I found my twin who grew up with me, I wonder where he is? what is he doing? "

Me: "what happened to him? You two were always together, how can he go missing leaving you all along? ".

Saken: "I told him not to, but he was too stubborn and worried after having a tour of this earth and looking at the hard non-degradable enemy, he went with an army of ours to gain immunity to fight all kind of plastic on earth."

I was shocked after listening, and I couldn't face Saken and tell the truth to his face. But there was no other way.

Me: "you better forget him and take care of your family".

Saken: "how can I forget my own brother, and what do you mean my forget him and take care of your family? What happened to him?"

Me: "I don't know how to tell you, you should forget everything and halt his search".

Saken: "tell me the truth or else I will kill you here "

Me: "if you want the truth so badly, I will tell you what might have happened to him".

Saken: "better do that".

Me: "the enemy that your brother was talking is non-degradable, even if your family invest a thousand years, you won't even reach the beginning phase of its destruction."

Saken: "if that's the case, then let me search my brother and bring him back".

Me: "I think you gotta listen to the whole truth before making any decisions".

Saken: "what's that?"

Me: "your enemy, is not just a common litter thrown by humans, it's the kind of plastic they end up throwing into dumping ground which in turn enter the Soil and most of the time that plastic enters the ocean. Which means your brother at this time might be dead inside the polluted Soil or inside the body of some marine animals. "

He started weeping as if the sky has fallen on his head. It was hard for me to convince him of the facts, but the facts are always facts that don't matter what. It's good that Nature gave every animal the ability to forget stuff after some time. I left the whole case believing that one-day forgetfulness will conquer his brother from his mind.

All you have done throughout your whole life is to acquire the piece of land and dump it with thrash and calling the big ones as "the seven wonders of the world". let me remind you of the real wonders of the world

The forest, which takes care of crore of beings
The Soil, which gives rise to many trees
The breeze, which fills life to these animals
The sunshine, as a kiss
The water, to live upon
The twinkling stars, as entertainment
The rainbow, showing out how colourful the world is

A crow takes care of nightingale's eggs believing that as its own throughout its life, but Nature is not a fool to take care of you till the end, the day will come when Nature smash out the growing egg of humanity out of its nest.

The air of superiority is really monstrous. The consequences are at the doorway to utter dystopia. Better late than never, I have finally liberated.

Humans ought to learn to love, live, and let live until the planet witnesses safety and freedom for all living organisms. Its better reserve your day of work on your environment to clean the littered plastic otherwise you would be the next to lye there.

◆ ◆ ◆

Once upon a time, there was a king
With a heart flooded with kindness
Divesting himself to everyone who stepped on
Donated is wealth forgetting sin and status

The more he gave, the more it came
That his life went till eternity
Salvation and habituation was his only job
memessing the world with treaty
He changed his colour from place to place
But his support stood the same
He took all the weight forced upon
That his strength couldn't be undermined

Bad day it was that the king saw a plastic
Which hunted him like a ray of sun
Unable to breathe and reach towards the air
He was helpless, his name was Soil

THE DOPAMINE BOMB

"Humans are attracted to the fantasy of forgetting the fashion of fabulous nature."

-- Poliovirus

Y ou, humans, are so fake that every time I try to analyze you, there's always something less, your cooking is fireless, your clothes are sleeveless, your relationships are meaningless, your attitude is careless, your feelings are heartless, the babies are fatherless, children are mannerless, education is valueless, the young ones are jobless, the leaders are shameless, the politicians are worthless and being arcane with these words I have become helpless.

Every time I try to have a glance at your face, I end up humiliating my self by ignoring the rule that your face is meant to be bent down every time staring at your rectangular luminous screens. Won't your neck hurt? Will you ever greet the one in front of you? Or are you humans evolving back to become gorillas? I wanted these answers, and the only one who can help me with this exciting exploration is Astrocyte, the bacteria who stays inside your stupid brain. I always wanted to know about a human brain, the organ procreated by Goddess Nature, sophisticated especially for humans, the organ which holds all the reasons behind your arrogant and ignorant behaviour.

It was one hell of tracking to get inside your brain, but once I entered your heart, I was directly there as more of your blood is consumed by your brain. On the way towards the brain through your red blood, I got this insane thought as I heard you, humans, advise your loser friends to "follow your heart". Wait! Are you mad? What do you mean by following your heart? Is it your pet dog to follow? As per my presence in your heart, I only heard it screaming Lub dub, Lub dub.

Finally, I was there, inside your spongy brain, it

took no time to find Astrocyte, who was there to welcome me, no wonder that he suspected my entrance as he was already the master of your brain.

"was it salty or sweet?" Astro asked without hi or hello confusing me

"what is salty or sweet?"I answered with a depleting smile

"the blood in which you came through"

"It was bloody disgusting just like their sewage water," I said, and he gave me a slight smile showing signs to my answer as a Genius.

"Which is that common thing that humans carry with them all the time and common thing that humans are uncommon to ?" he asked as if to test me again, and it was my time to maintain the status of Genius
"I don't know" I answered after a brief pause and started looking here and there to escape that awkward moment.

"It's their smartphone, that people are common to carry with them".

"what about that common thing that they are uncommon to?"

"It's their common sense, you fool" he answered and started laughing, falling on those grey coloured cells on which we were standing.

I was kind of intimidated this time, and I speculated that it might be Astrocyte who eats up human common sense.

"If that's the case, then what's the matter with this smartphone?" I asked to cover up the situation.

"It's not just the rectangular glass, there's a whole world which exists in there without even existing".

I was damn confused with this, but I didn't make an attempt to pursue more on this, as I wanted to explore the whole thing on my own. So I decided to stay inside the human eye and watch the smartphone and then return to brainy bacteria in case of doubts.

It was really a whole new world, the twitter, I earlier spoke of was not alone, he had some companions called Instagram and Facebook called as ShowOff medium.(Although you may call them Social Media, I am better in my own words.) After spending my precious time looking at your ShowOff media, I understood how vague you humans live inside as the virtual life instead of living the physical one filled with real emotions. One thing for sure, you humans are actually addicted to these showoff media. The place where everyone can be rich, a psychopath can be a peacemaker and the place where dead men live. It's no worse than your fictional hell rewritten as heaven.

 When the human I was residing on started to count the number of hearts below his own picture in the world of Instagram, I heard Astrocyte screaming for help inside the brain, I rushed out towards the brain to see what was happening, as I entered the brain, the strange situation was still taking its place, the Astrocyte was being chased by some strange fluid, the fluid which appeared like acid and it was so furiously flowing that itself explained how constricted it was till then to act in such a way.
Astrocyte was lucky enough to hang on to the top of the brain tunnel letting the fluid pass below it, I went on with some alkaline fluid collecting from your food pipe to neutralize the way he was hanging on.

"thank you very much, my friend, a friend in need is a friend indeed" he thanked by taking a deep breath and continued again "Did you observe the man counting the number of hearts below his picture?"

"How on earth did you know this?" I asked with utmost curiosity

"The fluid which followed me was Dopamine! Its Dopamine!," he answered, but the answer was still incomplete, and I had no patience to explore it by myself,

"Please go on to elaborate it until I say enough, do me this last favour," I asked, holding the power of saviour.

"It's not just an ordinary fluid, its entertaining fluid, every time the human-made a count of hearts and feel satisfied, the dopamine explodes giving short term happiness and disappears or won't explode during unsatisfactory results ."

"then what happens when it doesn't explode?"

"It gets sealed down by depression and anxiety, and doesn't program fairly, and during this time suicidal thoughts roam around the brain. And I remember myself inside the brain of mosquito once, it used to sit on a white powder called Cocaine, the brain of mosquito and its signs were as same as the state of this brain during the Dopamine hit".

I tried to understand the whole point, I saw many of you putting photos during my short stay in the eye, those of you were actually addicts, all the likes and comments calling that you were 'beautiful' were another hit of Dopamine inside your brain. When there's no satisfactory validation and attention, you can't get enough Dopamine, desperate you put another photo, and this cycle continues. In this process, your abilities are being misused and get mixed with random worms of depression which takes control of your action and taking away your motivation to be great.

Ants are addicted to sweet, dogs are addicted to mating, pigs follow the dirty way, and your brain has the great capacity to be addicted to anything if it has a potential to initiate even the minutest of pleasure even for a moment in time. Your addiction can be moulded to be good and bad, but tell me how many of you prefer your Books over Smartphones?
It was time for Astrophyte to go to his home, which was present between blood-brain barrier, I felt sorry for him, because of me he was forced to take the risk of an attack by Dopamine.
On the way home, I couldn't resist myself but to ask about the structure of the human brain to which he instantly agreed to answer.

"When I took rounds on the brain, I remember counting 1.1 trillion cells and 100 billion neurons, and a piece of brain tissue has about 100,00 neurons, and their connection to 1 billion other cells counts more than the number of stars in the sky."

"wow," I wondered and thought of taking a tour on myself around your brain after settling him at his home.

"But what about the thoughts and memory?" I asked

"Of course, I have a count on it, a human brain produces 50,000 thoughts per day with negative ones outweighing the good ones, and when it comes to their memory, humans nowadays are remembering the passwords to their showoff media more than memories" we both laughed, and we could see his home fast approaching, we accelerated with excitement.

I was back, after some time giving rest to Astrocyte, and began reflecting the day that went by, and thought about the biggest lie that I have ever heard in my whole life "you humans invented smartphones to save your time.". The science is said to be the extension of common sense, but by looking at your choices and actions, you would never reach to the extent of your full potential with smartphones in your hand swiping inside those showoff media. All you seek is attention with a steady internet connection, but not a good life and a steady relation.

I was surprised as well as shocked to know that everything was happening because someone somewhere was triggering you to stick to your screen and this someone was one of you again. They designed these devices in such a way that these devices have gained the ability to mine your brain so much that they ended up manipulating your purpose building mechanism. If I conclude in one sentence, it would be "Humans making another human, a smartphone and social media addict to make paper notes."
The devices have mined your brain in such a way that you have forgotten that it's always the hardships which give meaning to pleasures. Without those hard moments if you say "I experienced pleasure", the only chance of that bliss is some Emotion

controlling neurotransmitting drug. It's like having a delicious breakfast without brushing your teeth.

Once I got into the human laboratory through the blood sample of the affected one, there I was so glad to meet my friend Ebola who holds the record of being liberated twice on Earth.
Tears rolled down my eyes as I saw him and we both hugged each other, and after some gradual talk, he asked.

"Hey did you see those special humans anywhere who fly in the space called Astronauts?"

"How can I see them if they fly and float in space," I asked, and he gave a positive bright smile and re-framed him a question
"OK! During your rounds around the Earth, have you encountered any place called NASA or ISRO or something?"

"No! Everywhere I went, I saw 7 out of 10 humans smiling and dancing in front of memory capturing device, called camera, there were no Astronauts all I saw was JOKERS in every street".

"Oh, buddy! Astronauts are science people who can see the whole Earth from the place far away from here called Space, next time we get liberated, we will definitely go to space through their body and witness our Mother Nature from there".

"that' a great idea, I think it won't take long for our liberation again as these humans are stupid enough to liberate us as they go on killing our masters."

After my way out of there as I came out through one of the science men through his hand gloves, I came to know the reality of your ShowOff media through the story of mine.
I had more reach and infection on these showoff mediums than in the real-world, with false news about me, blaming for everything that I have done to you, but I am just going through my life process as blessed by Goddess Nature.
By the way, I don't care what you filthy humans think about me, because I know how you think and as I said earlier that I would take a solo tour around your brain, I completed it with heavy patience, this time, not just one brain, thousands of brains from thousands of humans

When I first stood outside your brain just below your skull, there were only tissue foldings, and it was calm and cool like an ocean, only after I went inside your brain, I found that it had a hell lot of noise. The scene was so similar to thunderstorms in between the ocean with darkness taking over all the corners with your neurons shining here and there every time you did some action of thinking. Different parts shined for different actions. It was a wonderful event for me to take a look at your action soon after your thinking

I know that you humans have two parts in your brain, the left part meant for logical thinking and the right part for creativity and emotional pieces of stuff.

But after my brief tour of your thinking process by different parts of the brain and the corresponding action it produced, I could categorize you, humans, into 7 types depending on the dominant thoughts by your brain.

1.The dumb brain: This is the type of brain which has no knowledge, but was initiating action of speech which manipulated the other brain. It means it was the brain of the brainwasher. Here only 1 out of 10 neurons made a sound and shined at the topmost layer, while all other neurons were under a deep sleep.

2.The God brain: This is the type of brain where all the neurons rested and as soon as they witnessed sounds of divinity or architecture displaying special signs that connected them. It's default setting was God, and some group of neurons overtook the whole brain leaving no space for science seeking neurons to come up.

3.The ShowOff media brain: This brain was slippery as it was always kept on getting washed by dopamine fluid, every time the person locked himself into his smartphone. It had no purpose making mechanism, all it had was its own future projection of getting famous like a celebrity.

4.The science brain: The brain where all the neurons were active and were always ready to turn up an accident into opportunity. It had no default neurons, but the human with the science brain always ran towards books every time the neurons were dull.

5.The psychopath brain: The brain which had misconnections of neurons everywhere spread around the whole brain. There were no clear distinctions in thoughts, but they were much intelligent than those of dumb brain and showoff media brain ones.

6.The money brain: Here there were logical neurons who overtook those of emotional ones. All it thought was money, money while eating, drinking, marrying, and dying.

7.The emotional brain: This brain always came out with a conclusion without rethinking, or it completely lacked the logical thinking ability of the money brain. It cried even at the smallest of danger and laughed even at the lamest jokes.

By the way, many brains were a combination of these 7 types.
Your brain's divided into two equal parts, do you know why? If it was a whole, you would be crying for a joke and laughing at a funeral. Everything is fine because you evolved like this. But still, the

glitches exist. Your brain is the smartest organ, but it is according to your own brain, not by anyone else.

You gotta come out of your perspective and think out loud before getting smashed by those wrong neurons triggering you to do wrong stuff.

Your brain is like a time machine, you can travel through time and space within a blink of your eye, but the problem is the time and place that you chose to travel back and forth. All you do is to remember the moments of pleasure neglecting those hard moments which had the potential to throw you above the average thinking humans.

◆ ◆ ◆

Tomorrow never dies
Yesterday never returns
Today may be the last day
Give good thoughts about its priority.

Every hour, minute and second
Many takes birth and many passes away
What's the point if you don't think a bit
Even dinosaurs lived their day

If the light was dark and water was hard
This world would be upside down
If fear was smile and sad was fun
Every moment would be your new dawn.

Live for the day you wanted
Love the day provided
Conquer every moment with honest
But do give good thoughts on its priority.

THE RICH, POOR GAME

*"Look deeper into Nature to be better,
your money won't be a saviour, only
when you reach your old age, you'll
understand everything better"*

--- Nipah virus

Rich poor game

You, humans, are obstinate. Each and every pro-
fession that you humans do to earn your paper
notes requires someone else to get in trouble. Law-
yers hope you get sued, doctors hope you get sick,
cops hope you're a criminal, mechanics hope you
have car trouble. But those who wish good for you
are locked behind bars as prisoners, the thieves are

the ones who wish prosperity for you. How ironic your money world is?

Goddess Nature made a man, man-made Money, and the Money made man mad. This story doesn't end here, as these mad money men changed the crowd go bad. The earth would be a better place to live without religion, countries and Money. Every one producing their own food for survival sounds way much better than notoriously snatching others Money by manipulation.

Million other animals are inhabiting the planet, and the one and only animals which die every day by starving are humans and the only animals which die every day by over-consuming are humans. Simply put, your world is now a money world, and this paper money is forcing every one of you to search for better perception instead of a better vision for the future of humankind.

You kill for Money, you cheat for Money, you even go hungry for Money. Remember that the food is free from Nature and until this time you never fought hard for food, you are throwing your sweat out just to put in some paper into your pocket dreaming about things that would make others go uneasy about you. The Money you possess attracts only the lazy ones around you, not the hardworking structured ones, if Money were meant to charm everyone around you, then the moneymen would have been surrounded by all the neighbours and peers all the time. You even named a plant as a

Money plant for satisfaction. Wow! That's a great tribute to plant kingdom.

I never thought that you would turn out so obsessed with Money that you would one day woke up to continue your daily work in pursuit of Money instead of your love and devotion to your work. This came until the extent that you ended up differentiating yourselves as rich and poor and decided your place to live, the quality of food you ate, the brand on your clothes and the place you get literate. The rich are just weak humans with some extra paper notes and clean skin and hair.

It was first brought to everyone's notice in a trial between a hybrid Dog which lived with Rich and the dirty Rodent residing in slums of poor.

It was a heated argument between that poor dog and the Rodent who went to trial in front of the chief justice of Nature. The judge was a Pigeon, well known for its peace and unprejudiced decision with no place for vagueness. All the animals were invited for the trial held under the big tamarind tree at the centre of the forest, it was the time when I was still locked inside my master Bat.

I know that you have even copied this style of bringing justice to the oppressed. Doesn't matter how fast the Young Lion runs and hunts its prey, it always brings down its head in front of its father. Just like that young lion you got to remember that whatever you have achieved in this universe, everything's inspired by Nature. The dams you build is inspired by a beaver, the helicopter you ride on is inspired by dragonfly, the arrogance of possessing Money is even inspired by the violent volcano spitting poison all around. You feel more despised when you lose money more than you lose friends.

The trial began, but the hybrid Dog and the Rodent were on their own without any advocate on their side.

"My habitation with Moneyless humans is not justifiable, I get to eat their dirt as they don't even leave a grain of rice. If this continues, my Rodent family will perish out of this earth without food. Honourable judge Pigeon. I request you to consider my request seriously and reassign my habitat like that of new hybrid Dog" complained the Rodent with a concern of its whole family in its words.

"that's my complaint to your Honour, I no more want to be a friend with Money filled humans who always feed me with artificial food taking my immunity like a robber. I have become an animal of experiment and entertainment. They force me to mate with some unknown kind of dog family. Which made me prone to human diseases" said the dog staring at the Rodent thinking about the exchange in their positions.

Every animal was tense and made an attempt

within themselves to predict the judgement as there would be an interchange between their habitation, but the pigeon was smart which took an exciting step to access their lifestyles and do a case study on it before getting to a decision. The responsibility of the case study was named to Bat wherein I was lying. Judge Pigeon chose Bat because it always woke up at night and could quickly get into any situation easily. All these improvements gave me an excellent chance to study you even before my liberation.

We visited Rodent first living in a tough slum with very little food in homes but filled with a lot of litter of precious humans.

We met Rodent at that very night over a bridge leading to the human toilets built above the sewage water drain, the place was very stinky but compared to your intestine it sticks less. I think there's a lot of poison in your own body compared to combined litter outside.

Rodent began

"these humans with whom I live with are very hardworking, and they get to eat food less than they need and whatever they eat gives them high immunity to fight us, they used to die of our bites in the beginning, but now they are immune to us. Sometimes when they entirely run out of food, they will never hesitate to eat us. Not a chance. We are in a great danger, Mr Bat. Just look around you, how messy their place is, two steps ahead of you lies their toilet and behind that room lies someone's kitchen. Still, they live without any fear of diseases. They don't care if I carry Hantavirus inside me or not; nevertheless, they will all hunt us one day and will succeed in making my family join to that of dinosaurs.

 Their health is their only wealth. They even stay without food purifying their gut in and out, you gotta reach this complete story out for pigeon and remember that the fate of Rodent family lies in your hand, Mr Bat."

Suddenly a human came running over the bridge holding his stomach hardly. He was running towards the toiled, confused, the Rodent, that thought that the man came to hunt him.

"Run for your life, I will meet you tomorrow at a new place" screamed the Rodent and jumped inside the human waste while the Bat flew up.

We couldn't believe that these humans are so wasted that they would eat a rodent. With this terrible experience, we never looked back. Instead, we turned towards the dog for the case study.

We met the dog inside the excretory room as the dog was not allowed to walk out freely out of its house. It was more like a prisoner but was called a family member.

You cage two birds and call them love birds, you pack fish inside small water and name it as Beautiful. How dirty minded you are.

The study began, and the Bat decided to stay with it for the next few days as the conditions were very much favourable with fresh air drifting around with a piece of pleasant music humming like a melody of paradise.

.

The dog began
"They don't let me free; instead, they are so cruel that these insane beings take me to their exercise room called Gym and make me watch them stretching their body. They eat hens and mutton in the first place and then to burn their excessive, unhealthy, disgusting fat, they hit those gyms, and I always lie inside the cage unable to sleep, sit and shit. All those with whom my family lives are mostly fat, Obesity is the disease found in 6 months old baby to the 60-year-old body. It is rising like cancer, earlier these filthy humans used to die of smoking now they are dying of overeating unnecessary food. I am telling this because, they feed me that food too, never bothering if I had ever wanted it or not. I think my family meant to serve Nature as detectives, but here we are rotting our detective brains inside these cages for nothing. Please help me Mr.Bat" called the dog and ran away as soon as it heard its master scream from the outside.
Our decision to stay there was demolished, how can we stay independently in such a place where the pet is prisoner.

It was the first time, that I felt respectful about my master Bat ,when he summoned the case study in front of the judge. He was unprejudiced, he was completely honest about both the species. He laid is words like a human philosopher would.

"your honour" began the bat "I feel honoured under the law of Nature for allowing me to conduct this case study on a hybrid dog living with rich humans and a rodent living with Moneyless humans. So here are my conclusions about them.

Both the animals deserved to have a better life, but compared to those of chickens, they are safe, the thing that is making them file a complaint is a non-living thing called Money that humans carry. A pessimist sees the difficulty in every opportunity, A optimist sees an opportunity in every difficulty but only A Money Obsessed could bring this difficulty in every opportunity . We can't undermine that these animals are waiting to free themselves out of their dreadful misery that none of us can understand. The victim here is not just a dog and a rodent; instead, it's all those animals who live in close proximity with humans. Humans are the once who needs to be punished, my lord. They are responsible for this insane development.."

The case study was finally submitted in front of the judge, and the decision was out from the pigeon who stated

"there is no exchange of habitat in any case as it would completely disturb the ecosystem and well being of all other animals including microbes living with them and when it comes to punishment to these humans…. "all animals raised their feet and erected their ears eager for the words calling punishment for humans.

"I curse the whole of Humanity
They may buy a bed, but they'll lack sleep
They may have machines, but they'll lack brain
They may have medicine, but they'll lack health
They may enjoy sex, but they'll lack love and faith
With every good thing they possess, they'll go on losing everything that made them a human being.
I curse them for pursuing Money and wealth and remain unsatisfied until the end of time."

Every animal cheered with their loudest voice possible with a sparkling smile on each of their faces. It was like Mother Nature reincarnated as a Pigeon.

A curse from the wise never fail, and so does this curse is taking over Humanity. From then on your life's been a rat race and when I look at an average person's life, it seems like how lost you are without any purpose other than working all day sitting at one place. Here's how most of your life looks like.
 You take birth, you are given a name and religion, you go to school with neat uniforms and shoes where your critical thinking gets suppressed so that

you can follow a pattern of an average student, you pass the school and move to high school, there you will focus on getting into college, and by the time you reach college, you would have forgotten playing in-ground and having friends. After joining college, you study the pre proved science equations with no use in real life just to take a well-paid job, then you get a job in some company, and you get money every once in a month. The money gets spent in a week on some shitty show off things, so you borrow money and to pay back that money you go back to work, and this cycle continues until you reach retirement. And by the time you'll be having kids and grandkids following this path and the time you sit idly in your home after getting old is when you realize what you'd missed all this time—exploration, learning new kinds of stuff and understanding nature at its best.

One day when I sneaked inside your factory there stood thousands of men arranging bottles of water beside the rotating machine, they earned enough money to have food, but they worked much harder than it is necessary. You know what? Cavemen were much independent that you are today. You people pay other people to live like a cave people on some mountain with tents calling it as an adventurous hike. How stupid!

The more you think you are advanced with Money, you are losing your freedom at an exponential rate. I have an idea for you, as you listened this far, I think you know how rusted your world is with all the pollution both mentally and physically, just run out of there and get inside some forest and enjoy the Nature at its best. Of course, you will get hunted by some animal, if it does, just die, that's what you deserve.

Business is the word that humans brought, Business is the culture that Money taught, rich and poor are its by-products. You, humans, do business, no animals, but you are affected. Everything is for sale in your surrounding, and even your life can be negotiated with paper notes. It was barter before, and Money made you cheaters. Money offers a glimpse at the cruelty of the world, of course, Humanity advanced with the encroachment of Money, but the problem took birth at your brain at your stupid mental pollution which holds reasonable for imagination. Its imagination all the time which gave you the most significant advancement leading to high power over Nature unparalleled.

This chapter won't end without the words of bacteria which stays on your Money all the time. He has been endangered along with me from the time you have started using those sanitizers.
Here's what he says.

"it appears like a regular paper, but runs from hands

to hands much faster than a good idea does, it's just a number with zeroes but can make a huge difference that it actually decides if a human will have food for his hungry stomach or not. Money is humans greatest invention along with books, but there's always one champion, and unfortunately, that's not books anymore, its Money. Money everywhere, there's Money in pants, there's Money in the land, and there's Money in love. We microbes and other animals are very blessed for not getting any chances to compromise our lives with Money, for Money would bring things necessary to live, what's the use if its the source of all the hardships, cruelty and destruction of Nature. Even human's imaginary God needs Money, the more I understand Money, the more I crave for it.

Finally, if I am glad to stay on Money instead of becoming Money, if I were, I would have murdered someone without even touching them.

This arrogant belief of advancement arising from the minds of humans won't stop until they realize that the Money is just an idea to buy commodity but not a medium to satisfy needs."

◆ ◆ ◆

Humanity is a fragile story
Weaved with paper notes
Humans are heinous actors

Tied with material thoughts

If Money spoke the story
Prejudice would lose its way
But humans went for the glory
Created weak under etiquette of gaze

Money can bring war and peace
Why not use it as ease
The problem lies in the imagination
Which blows cold like a winter breeze

The rich, the poor are all humans
With unsteady mind craving for more
The ape, the dog, are all animals
With no money mind, living like a lord.

THE FAKE PREACHER.

*"Mass media has more control over
human life than their parent's do"*

-- Hantavirus

The fake preacher

You, humans, are highly sensitive and. I have been into many human homes, the only common thing I found in every house was a big smartphone with small-sized people sitting inside with well sewed and clean clothes overreacting, spreading anger and procreating depression by collecting and presenting all the bad things happening around them. It's was the news channels through your TV.

◆ ◆ ◆

He was not at all ready to give up, there were no signs that he would lend his ears even for a moment and understand the argument shot by his opponent. He was totally immature and adamant but was called as an Expert with a name board in front of his desk.
Suddenly the TV went off, and a small kid of age around 10 or 12 rose up from the sofa he was sitting on and complained his father on account of turning off the TV in between a heated debate.

"don't you worry about that son, anyway these debates happen all the time on TV and just like you can't see the viruses around you, these people on the news will never reach the conclusion doesn't matter how long they discuss," said the father patting his son's back and I was shocked to hear about the virus his son couldn't see. Did he saw me watching the news with them? Did he have ultra zooming lens on his spectacles? Finally confirming that it was a pure coincidence, I moved on, and as I was about the leave the place, I heard his father advised his son about something.

"Remember this my son, Trust only those who have bigger library than a TV," he said and left the scene.

This wisdom of that person purely depicted him as a man of Science. The man who would never accept a piece of news or a phenomenon until it is true, the man with books and love towards fellow beings.

This whole incident gave me a quick task to observe every one of your homes just too see the size of the TV and library. I decided to ask help from rabies who would carry me through most of the houses as dogs are your favourite pet; he really helped me a lot.

After my brief investigation, I found where you humans went wrong with your mindset. It's filled with shit from that TV. As I took that science man seriously, I watched every debate possible and this is my unfortunate conclusion. Until that day, I never saw a single discussion on TV which emerged with a proper conclusion satisfying all the parties who sat screaming towards the camera with multilayered makeup over their face. Even those so-called experts were bound within their self-proclaimed constraints, no matter what they spoke, it always turned out to be entirely irrelevant for the other person. Along with this weakness of harnessing narrow mindedness and lack of perspective, they pursued even more weakness just by not listening to their opponent. The whole show looked like a bunch of morons fighting for a banana which has long been carried away by ants. Wait! Why am I insulting morons here?

From then on, every time I peeked at the TV, I was aghast as I was demonized and I was mixed up with lament all the time. Why? Why will they do these things? Why is news so obsessed with exciting and intriguing bad lousy news about their surrounding instead of discussing the goodness of nature? It was not just me who wearied, I have observed even humans went in fear most of the time only after listening to the news for 10 minutes. I could no longer take this, I wanted a solution for it and for that I got to find someone who can tell me what's being said about my whole family from these days and why were they doing so?

Here's how things work,
Today's news: "A plane named A-606 flying from Bangalore to Sydney has landed safely",
Today's news: "Breaking news! Everyone dead on a loud flight crash!"
Where did your attention flow? Is it the first news or the other news?
Of course, its second one, because it plays with your emotion called fear.
You humans can easily be triggered with three emotions love, hate and fear. With my presence in your neighbourhood, it was a daily routine for the news tellers to spread terror in these TVs.
When I was ferociously looking for my answer there was no microbe to answer my question (except that Astrocyte I met earlier, thinking my presence would lure his hope towards his life) and you were

the only ones left, and I can't just ask you ignorant pricks with big TVs for my answer, I preferred the books that your best brains have written, I have heard that to interact with the best brain is to read their book. When I remembered the place called library written over it, I flew in directly. There was very few people sitting with their thick glasses on, but there were many of you on the coffee shop infront of library with a slim luminous screen on their lap with a wire sticked inside your ears.

I wanted facts, the facts about this hatred news, as I wandered throughout the library I didn't find any books, most of the books were about your fantasies from writers imagination, I was so determined to find the answer, I took another round around the library. The library was coming to closing time, and all the readers rose from their seat, and among them, one directly came towards me and placed a strange orange coloured book over me, and as I was stuck inside, I crawled towards the first page and managed to read the title over it. FACTFULLNESS! Was written over it.

Guess what, I was fortunate and felt on top of my life when I read the book. I can't wait to share how stupid you are to get emotional and consume the news spoken by people with a paralyzed body.

The news channels give a lot of exposure to that

news that is really disturbing and can withhold your emotions with it and can catch your wandering attention at one corner. Attention is the currency that is taking over humanity. There are many may of you living on earth today employed through telling the news, its always been your nature to dominate and in the pursuit of this dirty dominance you are all ready to do nasty things. The reporters covers mostly that news which can liberate your mental agitation, i.e. sad and depressing news. If news tellers don't do this thing, they would be out of the TV and run out of their lifeline called money. If you were attentive and have some intelligence, you might have observed them announce the number of deaths with stress and to those who discharged with no importance. You must remember that there is a lot of good happening in the world than bad things.

Truth doesn't matter to them. All they want is victory. There are many instances that these news channels are disturbing your belief system by manipulating it in a very uneasy way. They frame every incident as a threat to human society, from slipping on the banana to a thunderstorm is being portrayed as a future threat for you humans.

A cat and every other animal except you lives in a dual reality, i.e., all they can witness with their brain is their surrounding(rock, plants etc.) and their senses(love, fear....). But for you it's different, instead of dual reality, you humans have gained a new reality—the stories. The world is dominated and influenced by the stories you tell to each other. This is the single most differentiator between you and other animals. The story you say has the ability that Goddess Nature lack. The ability to play with your free will.

A story can make a world a better place, on the other hand, a wrong story can turn this world into a graveyard. The news channels you watch have a firm grip over these stories and what they show is one side story (what they saw and came on camera), not the whole point, and you viewer give up all your time just to sit and analyze the story that is shown to you. If you know me as your killer, it means your mind is manipulated that you had missed the more significant part of the story. I have cleaned the environment reducing your carbon emissions for which you might have taken over 10 years, I have re-united families during your lockdown, I have given the idea of how a new member of virus look like and most importantly I gave you much-needed immunity.

You, humans, believe in what you see with special effects over it, disbelieving the less effective presentation.

Today except for Goddess Nature everyone is

biased, even I am biased, and everyone has their own perspective towards my outbreak, but it's important to trust those who tell the truth first and then their personal view, instead of these mainstream news tellers inside the TV. I saw many individual humans on streets with camera and mic interpreting news as it is. They are ones of Science and facts. The fake news you go through every day creates real opinions with real actions which ultimately leads to real consequences.

News tellers are so obsessed that they don't care what might be the impacts of their news towards Nature, they will be the ones to say about conservation of the environment and they are the same ones busy promoting the luxury wooden furniture.
Media can trigger wars with their elaboration and explanation style, they are up to propaganda, not the news. They made a lot of money when I was around, and they always came out with bits of information and then tried to conclude the whole story and hence manipulation of viewers and situation happens together. They told that the resistance against me was ready, the vaccines were getting prepared even when I was an epidemic, and there I was waiting for a vaccine against me even after I was a pandemic. Truth doesn't matter if they are winning by false promises and falsehood.

This is just the story of your reaction physically, do you have any idea what happens inside your precious brain while watching that overhyped news. I almost forgot the 8th type of mind in the previous chapter.

Its the Manipulated Brain: The brain which jumps to a conclusion doesn't matter what the credibility and concreteness of the news is. The brain which lives in chronic tension and connects with a series of disturbing activities from past experience every time it witnesses some bad situation.

I came to sneak into your brain without letting Astrocryte know my presence, everything was visible, the news was just like the sugar and fat to your body. The less it stays, the better, otherwise you'll be prone to depression, anger and anxiety just like diabetes and heart attack that happens due to high intake of sugar and fat. Your brain actually assigns some bunch of neurons as risk neurons, their work is to create a risk map and keep your body to be attentive every time as if under risk from a meteor attack or a terror attack. These risk neurons take over your brain and keeps your physical body like it was about to witness a smash by an axe over it.

The news you consume is very irrelevant to you, which really make me believe that you are dumb enough to watch some alien from a faraway planet sitting on a toilet seat. You, humans, worry about something that was never your duty to worry about, let's say that alien on a toilet, what difference does it make to you, if you watch that news? Are you under serious study on calculation the amount of time an alien spend on sitting on the toilet, or do you want to calculate the components of its poop? Just grow up.

I feel sad to say this to you, but, every time you watch the news, I saw stress hormones to come out and acquire your brain inhibiting some substantial growth of your total body. Some of you even stop growing mentally, and the development of your body begins to halt after consuming worrisome news most of the time.

Do you even remember that your average life expectancy is around 80 to 100? if so why on earth are you wasting your time on your smartphones and TV news like you have a lifespan of a tortoise.? Come out of your home and worship Mother Nature, you got far more mysteries to solve about it, even if you take next 100 centuries. Still, 90% of your understanding of Nature will be void.

It was all coming to an end, as I was about to leave your homes and get retired from watching Television again and decided to close my eyes and ears every time I see tv in front of me, then a whole chapter opened up when I saw an African woman turned herself into a White American after applying some cream. How did this happen? I thought that the cream is super scientific invention by humans till then. But I was dumbstruck to know that was actually an advertisement made by some cream selling humans. It doesn't end there, I saw far more surprising stories over the commercials. A man, after eating some mud-like substance from a small packet, gets so much motivation that the next day he was the owner of the luxury cars and big mansions near the ocean. And your smartphone was totally out of the limit of anyone's imagination, you can click the image with an ultra-zoom that you can even zoom the camera towards the mars and capture the wedding ceremony of aliens with ultra HD quality.

I thought that these advertisements were actually competing with the news channels in terms of stupidity. One of the most significant discoveries done by my favourite science people is the ignorance in the minds of every human, the more they try to extract dumb ones from ignorance, the more they get incepted with it from the hard work of this TV channels.

Freedom is a vital thing to survive and fulfil our lives with our dreams, but I believe that that freedom to change stands high than just enjoying freedom. Nothing is permanent without change, even the privilege won't last if we don't change, to bring this change we need to go under choices, and there are always two types of choices, the choice which initiates positive change that broadens ones understanding about Mother Nature and a choice which make everyone settle for something less than their ability. From smartphones, missiles and TV channels, these choices will give you a wrong place in world history. History has always been unjust to animals and the time is ticking, and it will bad for you humans too.

You, humans, are intelligent enough to eat and sleep but not to think critically and analyze what's the truth and what's fake is, even if aliens attack humankind, I would suggest them to attack by conquering news teller. Because you would believe if the news teller tells you that "the new alien invasion will be friendlier and aliens are here only for just an eye and a kidney out of your body."

There exist a lavish peace
Where there's no arrogant news,
You're stuck inside the cabal of fear
Ardent and fatuous without clues

The earth would still rotate
If they still folly
He nothing wrong with the world
But they still folly.

There's no base and depth in their words.
All they do is circus behind their desk.
The play where the viewer gets shocks
And the day turns into dusk.

The drams runs every minute a day
Converting truth as rude
You're stuck inside the cabal of fear
Ardent and fatuous without clues.

IT'S MISSILES NOT MICROBES

"Wars advances humans with destructive weapons, but not with the world peace"

----Salmonella.

Missiles not Microbes

Y ou, humans, are on the path to be friable, and for this thing to happen, there's no need of my infection contributing to your dark fate. You are your own enemies. Do you know what time is? Time is not just a physical quantity measured concerning space. Time is everyone's reminder from birth to death that doesn't matter how much you eat and how many you reproduce, you'll always end up getting mixed with soil consumed by microorganisms ignoring your colour, sex and riches. You are so busy trying to find a way to join heaven above the earth that you have almost forgotten that you can actually create one at your own place by achieving harmony with Nature. But compatibility, according to all humans, is just fictional like a guy called Harry Potter from a book. I heard you teach your kids to follow those who follow peace and the next movement, you will end up beating the same kid for biting that pencil, saying that God will punish you for your sin.

War is in your blood if there's one sentence to define human nature, it is best exemplified by "WAR FOR NO REASON".

◆ ◆ ◆

My family along with my friends' bacteria have already witnessed this stupidity earlier, in 1918

Spanish flu, Machupo virus on 1967, Ebola in 1976, HIV in 1981, Hanta in 1993, Hendra in 1994 followed by Bird flu, Nipha, Sars and Myself.

Till the birth of humanity, your own missiles in the name of protection have killed many animals on earth than we Microbes ever did till the birth of time. During the attack of my Grandfather i,e during your World War 1, which happened because of some lines on the world map created casualties of deaths by 105 million while we viruses altogether won't even come close to these number. Let me repeat it, YOU ARE YOUR OWN ENEMIES. Spanish Flu said that "You don't need to be a better virus to kill a human as real illness already exist in their thinking style". He predicted dystopia then, I think the post-apocalyptic world is your current affairs.

Not just the world wars, you are such an immature beings that I witness you people fight in the name of the land, religion, water, air, drug, alcohol, cigar, marriage, job, internet, fame and finally money. One more thing, there's a strange ritual of killing yourselves through hanging from the ceiling or eating some poison filled with bacteria, you call it a suicide, that's great, I do support that ritual, and instead of calling it as an act of suicide, I recommend it to be the act of Balancing ecosystem. There is no other animal on this planet which kills itself because of some grain-sized problems like, getting less sugar in tea. And I sincerely suggest you kill yourselves by hanging or falling off of the building but don't eat poison for it would kill some bacteria's inside your body forever.

I think this is the reason that Goddess Nature never locked any microbe in a human's body under a curse, for it would get killed by a random thought for suicide. If there's any animal that can protect microbes with its life, it's definitely not humans.

Every animal fights for its right, but not against its own community, except you, the word community never gave the Meaning of humanity.

Since the dawn of your evolution when your ancestors still had that undeveloped brain, they pointed God for every non-understandable situation, beginning at the lightning, ending at religion. I roamed around and even entered you Churches, Temples and Mosques. After that, a lot of time listening to your prayers and preaching, I found an interesting thing. Everything they thought was two types of knowledge. Ethical knowledge and Factual Knowledge.

The ethical knowledge is the one which teaches you how to live, its the best form of teaching that must be presumed to each and every one of you, it had depth in it. By saying "the pursuit of happiness and richness is the root of all evil", a Buddhist can change the material world into a beautiful place. By saying "all animals have their own life, none must be harmed by eating them" a Jain can bring harmony among all living life. But the problem sprouts out at their factual knowledge saying "their God exists and he is the only true God who is the reason behind all the sufferings of the world". This small statement has changed the history for bad. Ideas change the world, only when they change their behaviour. This time these facts with religions brought an unfathomable change in the behaviour leading the road to pursue superiority over others and this was the reason most of the time for the early wars when the science conforming all humans are apes was still a seed sprouting under the soil.

From the birth of humanity, you humans have witnessed my family and even fought us and many a time developed yourselves a better immunity. But there is strange insanity lying inside you, even after being moral animals you people fight within yourselves without any valid point. I heard that the countries that you live in are said to be the greatest inspiration for your fight, just to prove your superiority, countless of you die throwing deadly bombs and disturbing the fellow animals with you, and this is not at all acceptable. Ebola once told me that you used to kill trees with explosives so that these innocent trees won't help humans hiding behind them. And in preparation of bombs, most of your money is spent. Instead of spending money on teaching not to fight, i.e. education, you are actually investing money on training people to kill their enemy. If this is the case of conflict between countries, there are many unsung fights which often takes place within your landmass.

When I came out, I was almost afraid that these landmasses would unite under the name of humanity and would defend my invasion with proper treatment, but I was wrong. Despite my presence as a pandemic, there was a war between yourselves and some countries called India and China were actually fighting in their borders. Shame on you!. And those inside these countries were so busy counting deaths that they almost forgot my existence.

Heard you people even carry a weapon called Atom Bomb, which is said to have the capacity to destroy a whole landmass.

I believe that this Atom bomb of yours is the greatest invention ever made, and I clearly support that each and every country on earth should possess this Atom bomb as it would be the only thing stopping wars due to fear of destruction.

The ability to get fear was the greatest gift to humanity, as it drove your inner guts to fight in order to survive. Every animal has this fear, but remember that you are the only beings on earth who evolved with your mental state changing the phrase from Fight to Survive to Fight to Rule.

Just like your grandparents tell stories, we microbes hear stories from the Nature. When it comes to your history of war, all you did, in the beginning, was to fight for food, when food became feasible with the discovery of fire from the Nature, it united you people. The next step made you to fight for your people, then when the number of people grew, you fought for your common ideology, be it religion or race. They when you got split under your concept, then came lines between the atlas and the fight for countries began, by the time when everything got settled when we all thought that there would be no war from now, you started fighting to protect your preservatives thinking that you would live forever taking care of them.

One thing for sure, it was never the men of science who brings war, only the ignorant ones do, who don't understand the exact origin of Humanity.

This ignorance is killing thousands and lakhs today. War is the murder in the name of sacrifice. If ignorance is interested in Order, that is to maintain people, science is involved in power that is to cure the diseases. Many times I think that these Science people are cowards, hiding behind those ignorant leaders and following their orders to create a weapon of destruction. The time they speak will the day inaugurating peace around the world. By the way, your method of wars change with time, I have already witnessed the war with guns, the war with bombs and when I took rounds around your area there was a different type of war called as Cold war, the battle of upsetting others and yourselves to prove your point, even the tremendously educated ones among you does these things. If this is the case, the war ends only when humanity ends. You people are signed up from birth to give up the Meaning of life in exchange for power, let me tell you something obvious, We viruses and all the animal kingdom gave up power in exchange for Meaning. We serve our Meaning doesn't matter what. Of course, there are defects with every animal on earth, but the problem with you humans is that you attracted all those dangerous defects from all the animals. For example, instead of learning the ability to serve from cow, you follow a hyenas laugh. You eat like the crocodile, you look at others property like a Vulture, you disturb others like a Crow, you strike others like a snake and your body language resembles like that of a Fox with a smile.

There are no souls, there are only traces. Just like you have museums, we have sacred fossil fuels hidden inside the Nature. This statement is actually given by your own science people, and I must tell you that the animal kingdom has a high debt to pay back to these science people. The reason was the Virus which went Rogue. I feel ashamed to tell you his name, he is Rinderpest. Yes, the same member of my family who infected cattle and many other ruminants. They were the days of great shame for our family, killing many innocent animals for no reason. The story goes back to his first fight with his grandfather Measles. Measles ordered Rinderpest to kill the worms eating plants in order to produce edible food for cattle and herbivorous. Rinderpest was always arrogant like you, when he entered those pest's body to stop them from eating leaves and grass, he got sick and couldn't control the situation which gave pests an excellent opportunity to build up immunity, and when this happened, Rinderpest became a laughing stock in between virus family. This made his so nervous, that he was determined to prove to our family by taking a wrong step of infecting cattle. We couldn't stop him as he was so fast and effective that he had already infected and killed many domestic buffalo, antelope, deer, giraffe, wildebeest and warthogs. His infection was about to bring significant damage to the ecosystem as the animals like Lion, who depended on these infected animals went on without proper food. The whole system was about to get upside down, and when all the animals prayed for Nature, the science people came up with a solution. Today Rinderpest is no more. May his trace rest in peace.

Nobody learns a proper lesson without getting harmed a little. Would you keep a caged Lion in your house as a pet, you won't even if it's caged. Not because that you can't feed it, but because of fear thinking that it would escape one day and attack you. If this is the case, then why are you living around those poisonous smoke emitting factories and deadly Dangerous Nuclear Power plants, they are million times more lethal than that lion. Those power plants can kill million species at once, but the need for power want's you to have. I am concerned not because of me, no one can kill a virus, even your vaccines can't as they just help in strengthening your immunity. We care because of our masters who took care of us for thousands of years, we care of Nature who is ready sacrificing everything for our survival. You gotta come out of your incepted brain and think like a mature man.

You people act like communist until you get rich, feminist until they get married, atheist until the aeroplane falls, philanthropist until you hold black money, racist until plastic surgery and an activist until you get attention. This is how I can explain you until the death of humanity.

There will be an end. Dinosaur died because of the meteor, Rinderpest was killed because of a vaccine , but I am goddamn sure that the end of humanity will be dramatic than any other beings on earth ever lived.

One beautiful day, I was lucky to find the trace of Spanish Flu and his confession after being a Pandemic. It was Ebola who told about his recorded confession.

Spanish Flu: My confession

I don't know why humans called me Spanish Flu; I would have been named a Global Flu.

I was responsible for the deadliest pandemic on earth ever witnessed before, the most dangerous in history, I have infected an estimated 500 million people worldwide, which adds up to about one-third of the planet's population and I have killed an estimated 20 million to 50 million infected victims around the world. During 1918, when humans finished their first world war, I was discovered in Europe, the United States, and parts of Asia before swiftly spreading around the world. During that time, the science people didn't have any active drugs or vaccines to treat or kill me. Humans were ordered to wear masks, schools, and theatres. The thing that went to my mind was really astonishing and depressing for me. As a member of the virus family, it was my duty to travel by infecting one body to another, but why humans? They haven't done anything to me but to kill themselves in their wars. I was never meant to harm them in any way, but Nature forced my action against my will. Nature didn't respond to me and didn't ensured my goals before I began as a pandemic, but when I realized that I was the reason behind thousands of orphans and widows, I was at the lowest point in my life. I waited and waited for the signs of Nature to give me my reason's for being a Pandemic, but the answer didn't appear. I was about to come to an end after a year of being a global pandemic. I silenced my wandering thoughts by saying, "Everything has a reason." I have great hope that one day the reason will find you and one thing's for sure. Many more of us will come and kill humans, but I believe that it is not good to kill someone without any good reason.

I request to all my family members cursed inside their master to take care of Goddess Nature and remember not to bring any disturbance in any animals on earth without proper reason. Better be a peacemaker all the time, but don't forget to be a deadly hunter when the problem comes to Nature.

◆ ◆ ◆

I was staring at the sunset

When I heard the gunshot boomed
There lied the deer, tranquil with bullets
Nibbling to its baby, its heart hefting gloomed.

The baby sniffed its mother
Being naive with a shivering body
When the blood acquired its toes
Fugitive tears joined the cruel melody.

Unable to move and tired of crying
Heard the human's frantic sound
Capturing eyes of its mother, one last time
Ran the baby, through the harsh thorny ground

Eyes bound by tears
Smashed the wood with its legs
There fell a baby deer, tranquil with would
The scene filled with lion and its hungry cubs

It's not the Nature, nor fate.
Brought this tragedy
It's a human all the time.

Bathed with blood red and greedy.

THE FUTURE.

Future is a time where Present Projects and Past Precludes while the Nature Wins.

-- HIV

There will be no animals, no trees, water will be acidified, clouds will be blooded, and the whole of Humanity will be rotting inside museums. The time when future approaches the present removing the past will be very dreadful to imagine analyzing by the present trends. The universe began from a dot and came to a point where it is functioning through the press of button dots. None can say accurately what's in the future, for time is the only true master, but my intuition points to something vacuous. The prospect filled from freedom with none to experience it.

◆ ◆ ◆

What is life?

This is the question you people ask every time your neck relaxes from the luminous screen looking at the sky while feeling like a True Philosopher.

From the moment I came on this earth, the whole of Humanity was under my serious inspection, I have compared you with other animals and even quoted you, humans, as, "Arrogant species with a bad and beautiful Brain." But there was something in you that differentiated from other species as a whole. It was not your ability to tell stories, it was not your consciousness, intelligence, or curiosity. It was something different. It was that difference that made you who you really are. It is the ability to experience, and get immersed inside those special moments with other humans by mutually reaching the state of happiness and peace unknowingly. When I saw a boy helping his mother, hes mother smiles displaying her blessings on her kid, the ability that makes you expresses the purest forms of love through your face. When a man stops a bus to help a running passenger behind it, the satisfaction from both of them was out of the universe, and when an old man looks back at his childhood, his feelings took him to heavens. These are moments that make you who you indeed are. Other animals do experience these moments. Only you can express them, releasing your goodness into the world of misery.

Finally, life is what makes these moments. Moments

of love, kindness, happiness, and ultimately, the moments of satisfaction.

But instead of embracing these moments with every step of your life, you took the wrong route towards autonomy. You are already dependent on your mobile so much that your virtual worlds giving you those dopamine hits turned out to be the game-changers controlling your precious choices. In the near future, there will be days when all the mobile addicts will be sent to Focus Camps for the recovery. I will be counting on this as this is happening for sure...

 The only thing that remained with Humanity from its birth is curiosity. Curiosity is what made your ancestors acquire and rule over the complete landmass on earth. But this curiosity gradually developed in such a way that inventions towards the autonomy of life became a simple act of ideas. This brought in a drastic change to you and to your environment. It all began with fire. You replaced raw meat with burnt one and then came to your weapons made out of stone tied to stick, which gradually evolved to iron, steel, guns, and atom bombs. Your ability to fight physically vanished when your computers came in.

You replaced horses as vehicles. Then came your cycle, which totally transformed Humanity being an Extention of the human body. From cycles to cars to trains to aeroplanes, which can take you to each and every corner of the earth. This wasn't enough when many died due to diseases, so your curiosity towards medicines replaced and weakened your immunity given by Nature. When this happened, you sought more autonomy that the only thing left to replace was your ability to think. Today you have Artificial Intelligence. When this didn't give you satisfaction, you even went on the following curious path to replace your ability to imagine by inventing Argumented Reality.

Evolution is what made you complete, but your curiosity to explore and invent has made you imperfect. If each and every action of yours is automated, there's no need of you on this earth even if you want to stay; evolution won't let you live peacefully, for it poses dangers at every moment. Even if your curiosity will make you fit and convert you into a superhuman with all the artificial power to guard you, remember that advancements have come with a high price. You may have reached Mars, but you have forgotten that you could only explore 5% of the ocean, and when your curiosity takes you there, my family comes out attacking once again with a better offence like never before. If you take more than a year to find a cure against me, what about my family members frozen inside polar ice caps. You will never be able to make it out. There will be a day when Humanity runs out of fuel.

The moment you thought about automating your thinking ability, the end began. The human-made intelligence or the Artificial intelligence with which you humans feel proud of can be your dark fate. Behind every event, there is a cause and effect, but the creative brain always tunnels towards the right purpose and sound effects, and so it is happening with the procreation of Artificial intelligence. The world is still in the 21st century, and this non-living intelligence can solve the problem that humans couldn't even iterate.

You, humans, are perfectionists in maintaining good body posture, and you are already wearing plastics on your skin to look perfect. When it comes to the brain, it can't be moulded or exchanged with the good one, it can only be made inactive. One day you might be challenging turtles in terms of life span, but with very little decision-making ability, you will end up counting 9 as 6. Your bodies will be genetically engineered, if I compare today's humans with these advanced humans, all the future humans will appear in the same size and shape, pre-coded genetically till death that one will find difficulty in differentiating them. With this apocalypse, your clothes will be much smarter than you. One day your clothes will be the only ones to suggest washing your stinking body and eventually will end up cleaning you after being fed up with warning repeatedly.

What's ironic about you humans is that many of

your so-called intelligent humans already know these facts. And instead of thinking about it, they take their future as an entertainment inducer after making thousands of movies and writing lakhs of dystopian books on this. Humans are ready to fight for their religion more than their future. The future is predicted by those who create it, but human creativity is compromised, instead of working on art, you are busy building a machine that can create the artwork.

Lack of education will never be the problem; the problem will always be the human stupidity as most of you will never reach the line of competence and end up pulling each other's legs under the incompetence line.

If your artificial intelligence can tie up your choices and redirect your actions on the internet. They surely can understand your human brain more than Astrocyte, and if they can understand the game, it's quite sure that they will end up changing the rules according to its needs. If your machine gets the ability to be curious before attempting an action. They'll evolve and rule the planet just the way you did these days. There are chances that, the day will come when Humanity will vanish at one flow. The nuclear bombs will approach the land, the food gets poisoned, my family will be free. All that humans could do at this point is to run for help, help from their inexistent god. The moment they realize that all this time there was none, humans end up killing and eating themselves, displaying signs of re-evolution of homo sapiens, but this time the Goddess Nature won't make the fool out of her by letting it happen. By this time, the robots will be ruling over the land, sky, and water, terminating every possible threat. The robots will gain much from human invention, connectivity over areas, and the internet will immunize their ruling ability. And robots that are way much smarter than humans will one day colonize the world, but here's the catch. Robots are created by humans, and humans all these years were able to dominate on the earth because of their selfish genes, which promoted their survival instinct. If this instinct gets in the way of robots, they will all end up facing the same fate of humans creating themselves different types of government until one day they end up believing humans as their GOD and waiting for humans to return to set them free.

The earth is a drama set with the same story re-playing every time someone declares themselves as superior. The top problems belonging to the environment are not biodiversity loss, ecosystem collapse, and global warming, its selfishness, greed, and apathy. It's never the mystery to learn what it takes to know about the future. It's just the projection of present with some accidents in the middle.
Its time for me to prepare my family to face the future, remembering not to be selfish but to be sym-

pathetic.

Eat, sleep and run towards your office
Where you face your PC
With the monitor opening its eye
Feel the cold air from the mouth of AC

Its time that'll force you to eat
Not inner hunger
Its traffic that'll make you wait
Your enthusiasm's dead weaker

Away from the mountain and river
There you live in cities like ants
Following one another in a race for nothing
Replacing buildings with plants

Your tongue filter's empathy and gratitude
Bringing out lies of comfort
Your future beholds the darkness
Controlled by inorganic machines.

SOME HUMANS TO BE THANKED FOR

"Flowers grown in between thorny plants are always beautiful"

-- Marburg virus

T he night always gets followed by a Bright day, the bad always gets revealed through Good, and some of you got stuck inside me with your ideas and thoughts about the wellness of all living beings. A forest may be a dangerous place with all kinds of poison and poison bearing animals roaming around, but the forest is the same place that has that healers sitting around. Its time for me to praise and acknowledge all those healers of the earth who fell into my vision.

These are not the ordinary once; for ordinary means, those who eat, sleep, and reproduce. These are Ordinary people with extraordinary ideas putting some extra work to bring the best out of society they live in. "A change begins from within," said one of you, but the change to be seen is in the action we put. This chapter is dedicated to those action heroes, not the heroes of your movies but the heroes of Nature. Who thought that Humanity coexists with Nature and Humans are not alone the bosses of this world.

John Lennon: The music and art always separated you, and I still believe it is the only thing on the earth that you are exceptionally capable of executing even without being paid with that paper money. Your music and art can take you to the world unknown unknowingly; according to astrocyte bacteria, your brain will be in Elevated state that it is said to experience the utmost happiness.
One day I came to hear this song called Imagine sung by Jonh Lennon and thought that if he was the only human to experience the beauty and freshness of Nature. He was so remarkable with this song, that can actually mould the hearts of thousands of you around. He understood Nature so intensely that he imagines the world that exists without heaven, hell, religion, countries, greed, and hunger. Thoughts rise in mind, they give rise to actions, and these actions will bring real consequences. And imagination is the true God of ideas. I feel hopeful

every time I listen to this song. For hope has enormous strength that it can bring power in a weak.

Imagine there's no heaven
Its ease if you try
No hell below us
Above us only sky
Imagine all the people living for today.

Imagine there's no countries
It isn't hard to do
Nothing to kill or die for
And no religion too
Imagine all the people living life in peace.

You may say I am a dreamer
But I'm not the only one
I hope someday you'll join us
And the world will be as one.

Imagine no possession
I wonder if you can
No need for greed or hunger
A brotherhood of man
Imagine all the people Sharing all the world.

You may say I'm a dreamer
But I'm not the only one
I hope someday you'll join us
And the world will be as one.

This song dances in me forever till the end of the virus family on earth.
I believe if every one of you listens to this song with

real intent, no wonder the world will be as one.
If a song maker on your world is making riches through their song, it means their songs are being heard by millions of you. If this can happen, its a clear sign of revolution as it can bring an enormous change within the minds of millions of those who hear and embrace it with their unique hearts.
Nature respects John Lennon, and I would love to preach this song of him to all my family and friends. And he is not the only dreamer, we are with him . are you?

Picasso :
I saw people around the globe, releasing peacock under the flags of their countries, some saluting and some touching their chest. Why everyone chose pigeon? What does it signify? I thought and heard them say, "We stand for peace." were they joking? No, but pigeon actually represented peace around the whole world, isn't it a great thing for all the animals? Our supreme judge stands for peace. Inbetween symbols like the cross, Om, and moon star, a pigeon is representing peace. It was Picasso, the great artist among the humans who designated it. Artists are always found to be inspired by Nature, as Nature is the ultimate artist, and evolution is the ultimate art. If one can produce artwork inspired by Nature, it's like creating real magic as it contains all the strength to be immortal. Nature salutes Picasso for his thought, his idea for bringing Nature as the signifier of peace in between all your polluted arti-

ficial symbols. If all the artists, instead of just painting the trees with green colour, start to designate all the art of Nature for something good, nobody will touch and think about Nature with ruthlessness in mind. This idea of representing a tree, a plant, or an animal to something sometimes takes an extreme form where some of you placed rock under a tree and called it a place of god. I felt happy that your ignorance worked this time.

Charles Darwin: The heavyweight enemy of most of the religions today. If he were to be present today, his only way to live was to go underworld. Evolution is a scientific purpose; one requires an open mind to consider and accept this theory to appear as realistic. Evolution began when the first life on earth came, but you are familiar with it because someone broke the cage of ignorance by facing some of the most influential communities believing God. Although Darwin never proved the existence of Nature as a true god, as you people say. "the art contains the character of the artist." Evolution is enough to depict the enormous creative potential of Mother Nature. There cannot be another Darwin on earth, but many can come out of ignorance with his words of ultimate truth in his book I took note of "The Origin of Species". For most of you who are still wondering about the creation of Humans, it's always the evolution; it's better that you focus on reducing your carbon footprint instead of worrying about pre proven things.

Stephen Hawking: The man who daringly declared the inexistence of your God. What would you do if you see your kid following another religion rejecting the one you thought him throughout your life? Of course, you would try to disprove his belief in another religion; it will still take place doesn't matter if that kid is free to make his own choice. If this is your case, consider the position of all living beings on earth unable to express themselves. This can be done only by an extraordinary mind which is credible enough to bring truth to the world. This man has such an excellent reputation that when he died, all the animals around him were in grief.

Greta Thunberg: What were you doing when you were in school? Learning history about who killed whom or planning what will you be when you grow up? If this the case, you gotta learn from this girl; the girl who gave up her school sat in front of a government's building with a board daring to face the powerful money men of the world. Paper Notes always had the most significant influence around the world, it's wrong. Only true Grit and that intense look in the eyes of a fighter is far from above. Many of the parents force their children to school for what? To get knowledge of the world. What if the world doesn't exist when they grow up? Even if they live, at the modern plastic production and pollution emission rate, Nature won't be supporting their immunity to live life to the fullest. If a small school going girl can think like this, its time for you to follow her and join her hands, giving her the strength to fight for the betterment of Humanity.

They have always outnumbered the good ones. And the world will never forget them for their selfless effort towards the peace and betterment of the world. The earth is habitable because Nature exists, Nature exists because life forms support it too. If you take back the support, it's better to watch the graveyard with a forgotten name.

MY LAST WORD'S

Y ou, humans, are actually great! From building a roundly carved rock as a wheel to reaching space with solar energy, you have grown up. If this is the case, then defeating me is a kid's play only that it takes time. In the whole of Human history, Doctors always won, science has never seen defeat from its birth, all credits to your fabulous brain, which can control and monitor yourselves instead of running gipsy without any idea. You began healing the wounds, which led you to upgrade your immunity. You found fire, and today the light is at your fingertips at your switchboard. You adopted to increase your chance of survival, and today you are fighting to be immortal and become divine. No doubt that you'll be true one day. But all I plead you to take care of all the animals and plants around you, the infant is not just something that comes to your stomach, even a seed is an infant without its mother. Please plant! At least once in a lifetime.

You are not going anywhere other than earth at least for the next decade, please take care of our home until then, and by the time you change this planet, make sure you make this as inhabitable as before, who knows? Evolution can always bring in the next human from apes.

Problems define you much better than anything does, if staying on this planet is a challenge to you, and as you are capable of moving on to another world then you have that high power to bring back the earth to its original state, rich with trees and plants and animals roaming around like a king.

I have spoken a lot on your defects, ignoring your good nature so that you can determine where your glitch lies, take it positively, that's what makes you a social animal. If I have hurt anyone's feelings, there's nothing I can do about it, but to apologize, and I am proud of me that there was some truth in it. Nobody can hide their faces away from the universal truth. Its corona today, tomorrow someone else will raid on earth, and I wish that the upcoming virus or a germ won't get a chance to speak you like I had spoken in the pages before.

I wish you the best from the future because the

future belongs to you who are creating it every now and then with your advanced thinking ability; we viruses can't create a world like you, the only thing we can do is make you sick. Consider me as a messenger from Nature who tried to bring truth through the pain.

Author's note.

Every day thousands of books get published and millions are sold, but the book has it's effect and can bring change in the world only when the reader bring change in their behaviour. Change is the easiest thing to think , but the hardest to achieve.

If this book has brought some change in you or even if 1% of concern towards Nature has elevated, that's enough for me as an Author, it's been a very tough job to write this and it was very hard to think of a title like this, fearing every now and then if it would get rejected(If it offends you in any way, I sincerely apologize) . Every thing went fine and you have read this far. I am very happy about that.
It's still my first book, and I hope to write more in the future for the readers like you with many more interesting topics. For that to happen, your feedback really matters a lot, it can fill me up with enthusiasm, confidence and the much requred satisfaction.

You can reach me directly here:
Instagram : @pavanonwin
email: pavanonwin@gmail.com
Twitter :   @pavanonwin
Please provide your valuable review on Amazon, be it good or bad.

Thanking sincerely......Take care.....

Acknowledgement

I thank my friends Monday, Tuesday , Wednesday and, Thursday for standing still like a China Wall till the end of this book.

I thank all those who rendered support directly or indirectly for this book.

You guys rock!